Paul Johnson

Get Writing!

Creative book-making projects
for children

AGES 7–12

A & C Black • London

Reprinted 2011.
First published in 2008 by
A & C Black
Bloomsbury Publishing PLC
50 Bedford Square, London WC1B 3DP
www.acblack.com

ISBN: 9780713687750

The author and publisher would like to thank the staff and pupils of
Cheadle Heath Primary School, Stockport, for their help with this project.
In addition, thanks to Peter Linenthal for permission to adapt his lock
books on page 26 and 27.

The Book Art Project runs courses in developing children's writing
through the book arts. For details of courses and publications, contact Paul
Johnson at The Book Art Project, 11 Hill Top Avenue, Cheadle Hulme,
Cheshire SK8 7HN.

www.bookart.co.uk

Page layout and illustrations: Peter Gates www.petergates.co.uk
Photography: Stephen Jakub Photography, London
Printed and bound in Singapore by Tien Wah Press (PTE) Ltd

A & C Black uses paper produced with elemental chlorine-free pulp,
harvested from managed, sustainable forests.

Contents

Lucys book

THE PROJECTS

THE TEMPLATES

Enlarge the templates to 127% to create A4 templates

My Tudor House by Shaun (aged 7). Shaun made a rough trial on photocopier paper before embarking on the finished model. This model is from page 40 – Buildings through the ages.

Introduction

This companion to Get Writing! 4–7 (A&C Black, 2005) contains more than 75 new book making projects, many of which can be made using only paper and scissors. Exciting techniques, including lift-the-flap, map folding, pop-up and mechanical devices, will instantly engage 7–12 year olds. Research indicates that if children are involved creatively in the learning process their attitude to, and quality of work improves. The aim of this book is to infuse children with a love of communicating with words and images in the books they make.

The projects

This book is organised into different projects. Each project starts with a basic book making structure and then follows with some variations. While most structures are technically undemanding, the book projects on each spread develop from an initial idea, so that paper technology skills are developed gradually. Each spread also contains linked writing and illustration ideas. These range from narratives for 7-year-olds, to multi-genre challenges for older children. The illustration and design tasks are cross-curricular, from narrative illustration through captioned diagrams to map making and advertising. However, there are no rules about how to use this book. You can select ideas that are relevant to your planning, or that you know will attract the children you teach.

Showing children how to make books

First, demonstrate folding with the class watching, and then again with the pupils copying you. Go through the folding process slowly, repeating what to do at each stage. Some pupils will understand quickly and others will take more time. You could invite a pupil to become teacher and take the class through the first few folding stages. Suggest that the pupils do the folding in pairs so they can help their partner when it comes to any tricky bits. Always have spare paper at the ready for disasters and don't forget to reverse the instructions as necessary for left-handed children.

It is helpful to draw diagrams to support your demonstration and instructions. If you have an interactive whiteboard these diagrams can be saved for future use.

MAKING THE BOOKS — WHO DOES WHAT?

At times you may need to intervene in the making process, or take on some parts of a process yourself, but children should be able to say at the end of a project 'I did it myself'. There are situations when the time invested in pupil book making will seem too excessive and teacher/teaching assistant production becomes necessary. A compromise would be for you to do the initial folding but pupils to complete the folding or cutting.

ROUGH AND FINISHED MODELS

Pupils can make a rough model of their book or pop-up on plain A4 paper before embarking on the finished piece. Use the rough practice piece for preparatory work or let pupils take it home to share with their family and friends.

WRITING

Prepare the text with the book form in mind. If possible, pupils can draft in the first 'trial' book they make and present the edited text in the 'finished' version. Encourage older pupils to plan texts to fit the page. When a book has a finite number of pages, everything has to be contained within a fixed number of pages of a certain dimension — say, ten lines of text, with an average of eight words to a line. This is a useful discipline in refining and editing texts. With books of infinite length (e.g. the extended book on page 24) the pupil is free to write without limitation.

ARTWORK

When making pop-ups, paper mechanics and model theatres, complete all the artwork before the final gluing down process. It is difficult to apply artwork after gluing the various sections together. Most of the illustrations in the photographs in this book were drawn using pencil crayons. Coloured pens can also be used, but it is easy to ruin a beautiful drawing with over zealous use of fibre-tipped pens. However, fine black line pens are ideal for book illustration especially when combined with sensitive colouring. Avoid using paint as the paper may be stretched out of shape.

Hidden drafting books

Hidden drafting means that the draft cannot be lost but is hidden from view and can be instantly accessed for assessment purposes by both you and the pupil. A simple yet effective way of processing both draft and presented writing in one format is as follows.

1. Fold a piece of A4 paper widthways and lengthways. Unfold.

2. On the portrait or landscape orientation, pupils can use the top half for draft work and present their finished work on the bottom panels.

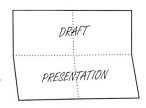

3. Pages can be added by joining additional A4 sheets at the back with a strip of masking tape.

4. When finished, fold the top half of the pages behind the bottom half.

5. Make a simple cover and tuck the edges of the first and last pages into the cover flaps to hide the draft work.

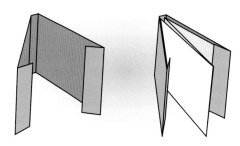

Materials and equipment

PAPER
Photocopier paper is suitable for drafting but it is recommended that you use good quality paper for finished work. See page 64 for a list of recommended paper types and suppliers.

PAPER SIZE
Paper sizes identified in the text are for guidance only. In some cases, the nature of the project itself will suggest the size of paper to use. Larger paper is harder to fold but can be easier to manipulate and work on when folded. The available working area will also be a factor.

Shipwreck by Barney (aged 9). Michael Morpurgo's Kensuke's Kingdom inspired this book. Pupils drew around a cardboard template 1 cm smaller than the page before starting. Illustrations were used to fill areas not filled by text. Only the finished pages contain illustrations and decorative borders.

Some projects require square paper or paper divided into three parts. Here are short-cut techniques for both of these:

CUTTING A SQUARE FROM RECTANGULAR PAPER
Align short edge against adjacent long edge. Where the corner touches the bottom edge fold vertically and cut along the crease.

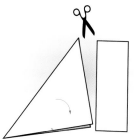

DIVIDING A RECTANGLE EQUALLY INTO THREE PARTS
Lay a ruler at zero on the left edge of the paper. Slant the ruler until the opposite edge measurement can be easily divided by three, e.g. 9, 15, 21.

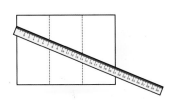

TOOLS
For most of the projects all you need is paper, scissors and, occasionally, rulers and glue. Glue sticks are suitable for rough models on thin paper, but PVA adhesive is best for thicker paper and pop-ups. Add specific project details. Pupils should use a ruler and pencil to draw solid lines to be cut and dashes to be creased. You can check that they are in the right place before cutting, and have erasers at the ready! Rulers can also be used to fold sharp edges.

DON'T FORGET TO ADVISE THE CLASS ABOUT SAFETY PROCEDURES WHEN USING SCISSORS:
- Keep the scissors shut when not in use.
- Hold the paper you are cutting below the scissor-cutting direction.
- Ensure that the scissors are not hidden under any pieces of paper while working.

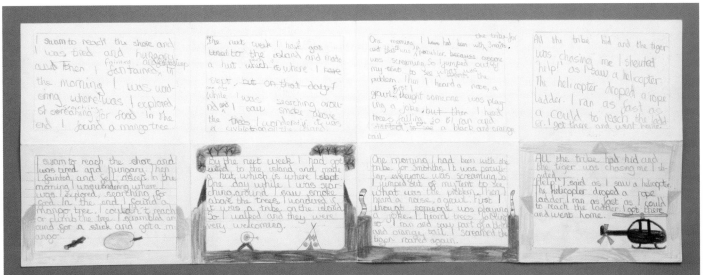

Making basic books

The zigzag book

Many basic books start with a sheet of paper divided equally into eight rectangles. The eight-page zigzag book (or accordion book) is the most common of these and the easiest to make, as it requires nothing other than one sheet of paper.

1. Fold paper in half widthways, from right to left (or the other way if left handed).

2. Fold top open edge in front of you to the middle crease. Turn the sheet over and repeat.

3. Open the whole sheet so that it makes a letter 'M'. Flatten the sheet.

4. Fold the top edge forward to the bottom edge.

5. Fold into a zigzag.

The origami book

This is the most popular basic book using the eight-rectangle method. By making a single cut to the basic zigzag book, and by using a different folding pattern, a fantastic three-spread book with a cover is created.

1. Open the zigzag book and fold it widthways in half. On the folded edge, make a cut halfway along the horizontal crease.

2. Open out the whole sheet and fold lengthways in half. Push the left and right edges all the way into the centre to make a cross.

3. Fold up the pages, as shown, to make the book.

In-house publishing

Another benefit of using a single sheet of paper to make a book is the opportunity to publish multiple copies using a photocopier. A class can produce a beautifully designed book in black and white or colour. Many computer printers also have a colour photocopying facility that allows you to reproduce an A4 sheet.

DESIGNING THE BOOK

The origami book has six pages plus a front and back cover. The zigzag book has, in effect, no back cover so the last page before the front cover can be an extra page for text or the equivalent of a back cover containing the 'blurb' (see below). Whatever the subject, books look more attractive with illustrations. Additionally, pictures and diagrams convey meaning that words cannot always deliver. Aesthetically, the page looks better if the margin at the bottom of the page is slightly wider than the one at the top of the page. Check how near to paper edges your school photocopier will print. This is important if you are planning to include decorated borders in the design.

DRAFTING THE BOOK

Fold a sheet of paper into the form that the finished book will take, and number the pages in pencil. A4 paper makes A7 size pages rather small — so it may be easier to work on A3 paper. Next, decide on the most suitable page presentation, such as alternating pages of text and illustration, or half page text, half page illustration.

Unfold the sheet, using the numbers to work out the order and orientation of each page. Pupils should plan and draft the six pages but leave out the illustrations. This does not necessarily mean that the text has to be in six parts as some pages may be full-page illustrations, diagrams or maps. Pupils should draw 1 cm page borders, draw lines for writing if required and draft the text in pencil. After editing, the book is ready for the presentation stage

Alternatively, you can provide pupils with a ready-made template. Give them one copy of the template for the draft, and another for the finished book. Two sample templates (including the one used in the photograph) can be found on pages 60 and 61.

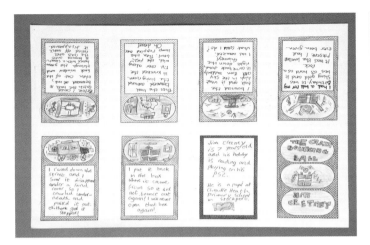

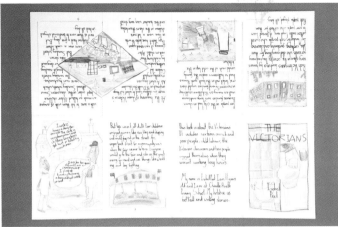

The Crazy Bouncing Ball by Jim (aged 7). This book master was created using the template on page 60. Note that the top half of the book is 'upside down'.

The Victorians by Isobel (aged 11). Isobel presented aspects of Victorian life in her project book. Most are single page entries but the school section has a two-page spread. She planned the pages integrating text with illustrations. The writing style is non-fiction narrative.

CREATING THE BOOK MASTER

It is easier to lay a book master on the photocopier if the sheet has no creases, so ideally sketch out the position of the pages with pencil and ruler on a flat sheet and complete the contents without creasing the paper. Write (or write over pencil text) in black ink – this will photocopy better. This also applies to the illustrations (unless photocopying in colour), which should be made at this stage.

For a more sophisticated book, pupils could design their own page format on a computer and word process the text (and create illustrations) on screen.

A selection of books published using a black and white or colour photocopier. Colour illustrations are 'tipped in' – that is, artwork is colour photocopied, cut out and glued into the pages. Black and white photocopied books can be enhanced by printing on to coloured paper.

THE COVER

Design covers carefully in pencil, with the title at the top and the author's name at the bottom. Then overwork in pen. Upper case letters often look best on the front cover. Reserve the central area for an illustration drawn from the book's contents. The back cover 'blurb' could contain a synopsis of the book ('This book is about...') and an autobiographical outline of the author. The school's logo makes an attractive tailpiece.

COPYING THE BOOK MASTER

Place the finished master carefully on the copier so that it aligns with the measurement indicators. Failure to do this may result in the copied pages not folding down accurately. No two photocopiers seem identical so make trials on your school copier to get the best results.

Making books and the curriculum

Book making is a highly successful cross-curricular approach to learning, employing a range of writing styles, art and design, and paper engineering techniques. Get Writing! 7–12 encourages children to use their writing skills across the curriculum and, as they do so, to develop these skills. This book includes ideas for many fiction and non-fiction text types. There are opportunities for making books connected with English, mathematics, science, RE, history, geography, art & design, citizenship and design & technology.

The table below indicates the subjects and topics to which the USE IT! activities in this book are related for children in Key Stage 2. All the activities develop problem solving skills. There are also opportunities to focus on shapes, measures and fractions.

Book	Literacy Types of writing	Across the curriculum Year, subject and topic
1 – Flap books *Cherile*	Biography, non-chronological reports, labels, non-fiction	**3 Science:** Plants and growth **3 Geography:** Weather around the world **5 Science:** Healthy eating **3/4 History:** Ancient Egypt **4 Science:** Animal habitats
2 – Traditional origami books *maby yes*	Stories which raise issues/dilemmas, traditional stories, non-fiction texts, persuasive writing, reports, recounts, poetry: language play, alliteration, information texts, character sketches and profiles	**3-6 Citizenship:** Choices **5 Science: Keeping** healthy **3/4 History:** Local community/family **5/6 History:** Victorian inventors
3 – Pop-up origami books *Mabey*	Stories set in imaginary worlds, developing settings, instruction texts, explanation texts, dialogue, character sketches and profiles, picture storybooks, captions, diagrams	**5 Science:** Space **5 Science:** Animal lifecycles **4 D&T:** Moving storybooks
4 – Amazing storybooks *yes*	Stories which raise issues, report texts, describing settings, biography, adventure and mystery, developing settings	**3-6 Citizenship:** Rules and laws **2 History:** Edwardian seaside holidays
5 – Our World books *Mabey*	Information texts, graphs and charts, report texts, re-telling stories, legends, maps, persuasive writing, lists	**5 Science:** Solar system **3-6 Geography:** Contrasting localities **5/6 History:** Exploration **4 Geography:** A village in India
6 – Decorative spine books *yes*	Recounts: diaries, report texts, re-telling stories from other cultures, journalistic writing	**3/4 History:** Second World War **5/6 History:** Victorian children
7 – Map fold books	Re-telling traditional stories, labels, captions, contents page, instruction texts, extending traditional stories, report texts, persuasive writing, lists	**3 Geography:** Mapping our local area **6 D&T:** Adventure playground equipment **3 Science:** Teeth and eating **5/6 Science:** Energy use in the home
8 – Never-ending books	Recounts: newspapers and magazines, recount texts, extended writing	
9 – Spine lock books	Lists, explanation texts, report texts, graphs and charts, information texts, captions, making a scrapbook	**5 D&T:** Musical instruments **2 Music:** Exploring instruments **4 Art and Design:** Investigating pattern **3-6 Citizenship:** Children's rights and responsibilities
10 – Compilations books	Report texts, comparison, labels, biography *and computer books*	**5/6 Geography:** Investigating rivers, investigating coasts **6 Science:** Rainforests and deforestation **4 Science:** Habitats **4 Geography:** Improving the local environment **3-6 Art and Design:** Famous artists

11 — Triangle books	Persuasive texts, report texts, symbols, character portraits, diaries and calendars	**3/4 History:** Viking and Roman settlements **3 RE:** Signs and symbols **3-6 History:** Medieval castles **5/6 History:** Victorian children
12 — Slot books	Persuasive texts, writing letters, stories set in imaginary worlds, character sketches and profiles, report texts, using known story settings, fact files	**5 Science:** Space **5 Science:** Animal lifecycles **4 D&T:** Moving storybooks
13 — Hinged pop-ups	Stories which raise issues, report texts, describing settings, biography, adventure and mystery, developing settings	**5 Science:** Life cycles of humans and animals **3-6 Geography:** Endangered animals
14 — Bird pop-up book	Information texts, speech bubbles, explanation texts, fact files, stories set in imaginary worlds, report texts, stories that raise issues	**4 Science:** Bird habitats, how birds fly **3/4 History:** Roman culture and symbols **5 Science:** Conservation
15 — Pop-up Greek legends	Re-telling myths and legends, promotional writing, stories with historical settings, developing stories with familiar settings	**5/6 History:** Ancient Greece
16 — Building through the ages	Extended captions, plans, recount texts, labels, developing characters, stories with historical settings, report texts, recounts: magazines, stories with familiar settings posters, re-telling traditional stories	**3/4 History:** Rich and poor in Tudor times, Tudor houses **5/6 History:** Victorian children **6 D&T:** Structures
17 — Fan pop-ups	Stories with familiar settings, recount texts, assembling information, labels, persuasive texts: posters, re-telling stories from other cultures,	**3-6 Geography:** Life in China **6 ICT:** Research using the Internet **5 Science:** Habitats
18 — Pop-up windows	Poems, reflective prose, re-telling scenes from known stories, promotional writing	**5 Science:** Seasons **3-6 Music:** Christmas carols **3-6 Geography:** Landmarks, tourism
19 — Story theatres	Re-telling traditional stories and fables, developing plot, characters and settings, plays, information texts, recount texts, promotional writing, formal writing, messages	**6 D&T:** Adventure playground equipment **3-6 Citizenship:** Conservation **2 History:** The Great Fire of London
20 — Paper mechanics	Lists, explanation texts, poems, re-telling stories with historical settings, science-fiction, writing letters	**5 Science:** Healthy eating **5/6 History:** Ancient Greece **5 Science:** Space
21 — Jointed paper mechanics	Journalistic writing, non-chronological report texts, promotional writing, assembling information, character sketches and profiles	**5/6 History:** Victorian toys **3 Science:** Teeth and eating **6 ICT:** Research using the Internet **4 Science:** Habitats of British birds
22 — Split level books	Developing characters, stories with historical settings, character profiles and sketches, information texts	**3-6 Geography:** Contrasting UK localities **4 Science:** Habitats
23 — Secret Garden books	Poems, developing imaginary settings, captions	**3-6 Citizenship:** Conservation **3 Science:** Plants
24 — Containers for books	Messages, collaborative writing (narrative and non-fiction)	Useful for presenting whole-class or group work
25 — Book stands	Poetry and single-page writing projects	Useful for presenting individual and group work

1 – Flap books

Lift-the-flap books go back to the 18th century and have been popular in children's books ever since. A project with lifting flaps is much more exciting for children than one without.

Make the single flap book

1. Open an A4 zigzag book (page 6) and cut along the dotted lines.

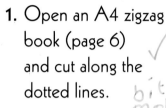

2. Fold the top flaps forwards.

Double flap book

1. Fold an A3 sheet of paper in half lengthways. Unfold. Fold each half towards the centre crease and unfold. Fold the paper in half widthways and then again and unfold. Cut along the vertical creases up until the first fold at the top and bottom of the paper.

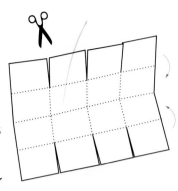

2. Fold the flaps towards the centre of the paper.

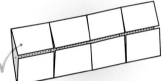

✎ USE IT!

- Make a 'Guess who I am' book. On the closed flap, write a description of a famous person or sports personality. Under the flap, write the identity and details of the person. If possible, attach a photograph of him/her.

- Make a 'Make a wish' book. On the closed flaps, write 'Wish 1', and so on. Under the flaps, write 'I wish I could…'.

- Turn the paper sideways. On the closed flaps, draw the root, stem, leaves and flowers of a plant. Under the flaps, describe the parts of the plant or stages of growth.

✎ USE IT!

- What's in the news? Ask the class to write a news headline on one of the closed flaps along the top. Write a short introduction on the bottom flap. Continue the news story in more detail under the flaps.

- Make a weather book for young children. Draw different types of weather on the top flaps and weather symbols on the bottom flaps. Write descriptions on the inside. Ask the class to consider what they need to think about when writing for a younger audience.

- Make a 'Super Salads' book. Write the title of the salad, e.g. Caesar salad or salad Nicoise, on the top flap. Draw a picture of it on the bottom flap. Write the recipe under the flaps.

Doors beneath doors book

1. Fold an A4 sheet of paper in half widthways. Fold in half again. On the cover, cut a large lifting flap.

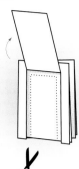

2. On the page beneath, cut a slightly smaller flap.

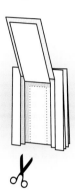

3. Repeat to the page under that.

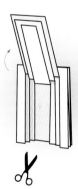

✏️ USE IT!

- Make Tutankhamen's burial chamber. Make door 1 lead to the antechamber, door 2 to the burial chamber and door 3 to the treasury. Imagine that the flaps are like layers of bandages on an Egyptian mummy. Draw amulets on the tops of the flaps and describe their purpose on the undersides of the flaps.

- Make an 'Animal house'. Each door can describe the habitat of the animal drawn on the flap. The type of animal could correspond to the size of the door.

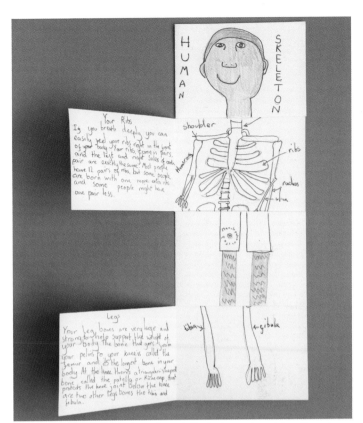

'Human Skeleton' by Anthony (aged 8). Anthony drew himself on the cover and his skeleton in four parts under the flaps. He describes how each part works on the undersides of the flaps.

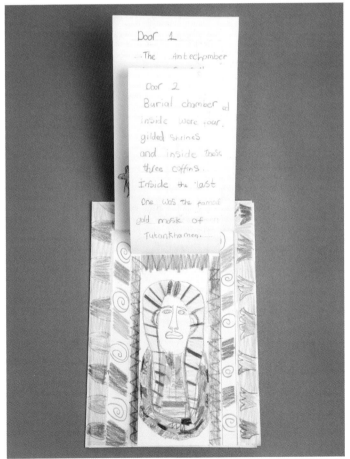

'Tutankhamen's Tomb' by Rebecca (aged 8). This project is an example of the first suggestion in USE IT! Each door represents a different room in the tomb – the antechamber, burial chamber and the treasury.

2 – Traditional origami books

Authentic origami books are made solely by folding and not cutting paper, unlike the popular origami book (page 6). You can also make pockets to contain removable information, which makes these books appropriate for promotional genres.

Make the basic origami book

1. Cut an A3 sheet of paper into a square. Fold in half and then in half again and unfold. Fold the top and bottom edges to the centre crease and unfold. Fold the left and right edges to the centre crease. Turn paper over. Fold diagonally towards the centre to make diamond-shape creases as shown.

2. Take the top, left-hand side and fold along the diagonal crease. Take the top, right-hand side and fold along the diagonal crease towards the left and fold flat. Take the bottom, right-hand side and fold along the diagonal crease. Take the bottom, left-hand side and fold along the diagonal crease towards the right and fold flat.

3. It should now look like this.

4. Turn over. Open out the middle and fold flat.

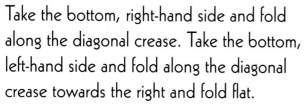

5. Fold in half to make the book, which has three spreads.

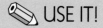

✏️ USE IT!

- Write warnings found in traditional tales on the pages. For example, what the 'Three Little Pigs' tells us about the dangers of badly constructed houses, or how 'Hansel and Gretel' warns us about the dangers of strangers. Each house could begin, 'Do not…'.

- Ask the class to write about and give reasons for things they like and don't like.

- Make a book about looking after your pet. Each spread can have information about what your pet eats, what vaccinations it needs. Add drawings to illustrate the text.

Four-spread book

1. Follow the instructions to make the basic origami book.

2. Fold the centre of the folds between the first and second spread forwards like a tent, making two triangular pockets.

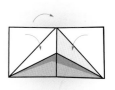

3. Fold book vertically so that these folds are on the outside to form the cover.

- Ask the children to make a book about their family's history. On spread 1, write about their grandparent's generation. Spread 2, write about their parent's generation. Spread 3, write about their own generation. Include family photographs on the final spread.

- Make a poetry book and explore alliteration, e.g. Lovely leaves in late autumn…. Add drawings to illustrate the words.

- Devote each spread to a living, historical or fictional person the children would like to be. Give reasons for the choices.

- Make a book about personal hygiene. Use the pockets to hold 'How to' information about bathing regularly or taking care of your fingernails and toenails.

- Make a book about five Victorian inventors and their inventions. Make a folded down diagram (page 25) of two inventions to slot into the pockets.

- Ask the children to make a secret diary for a character in a story they are reading. What can we learn about him/her from these entries?

Five-spread book

1. Follow the instructions to make the four-spread book.

2. Fold the centre of the folds between the second and third spreads forward like a tent, making two triangular pockets to hold removable items.

'Safety in Your Home' by Morgan (aged 7). Morgan has made a book about domestic safety room by room. The pockets hold important information, for example, the dangers of domestic fires and how to cope with them.

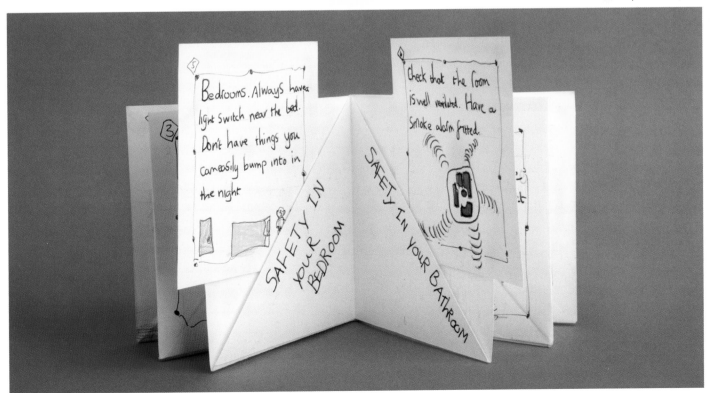

3 – Pop-up origami books

You only need scissors for this impressive pop-up book that in a flick becomes a flat piece of paper! Choose one of the three models below that is best suited to your class. Or, you can start with the first one and those who are ready, can progress on to the next one. You can photocopy the advanced model template on page 62.

Make the basic pop-up origami book

1. Open an A3 origami book (page 6) in the 'W' position. Fold the left and right edges to the centre.

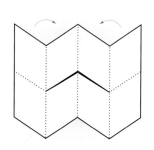

2. Cut half a house shape in the bottom left panel, half a rocket shape in the bottom right panel and half a planet shape in the top right panel as shown. Make sure you don't cut through the whole shape. Fold each shape forwards and backwards along the dotted lines. Unfold.

3. Re-fold the origami book. Lift the pop-ups so that they fold outwards.

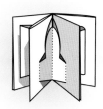

★ Helpful hint: Cut the pop-up shapes no further than half way across the page. The artworks can be drawn with the pop-ups flat. Also, remember that the pop-up shape on the top right panel must be cut upside down.

✎ USE IT!

- Write an exciting space adventure story for younger children. Tell the children that the challenge is to write no more than two short sentences per spread. Plan and write text first so that the artwork can be put in around it.

- Make a book on 'How to make a rocket'. The pop-ups can be used to illustrate preparing to make a rocket, taking off and landing on another planet.

- Make a non-fiction pop-up book, e.g. the lifecycle of a butterfly. Spread 1 can be the egg, spread 2, the chrysalis/caterpillar, spread 3, the butterfly. The children will need to work out what the pop-up shapes should be.

Add extra pop-up shapes

1. Follow the instructions to make the basic pop-up origami book, but make two pop-ups on each spread. Cut half a house and garden fence shape on the bottom left panel, half a rocket and clouds on the bottom right panel and half planets on the top right panel. Make sure you don't cut through the whole shape. Fold each shape forwards and backwards. Unfold.

2. Re-fold the origami book. Open each spread and fold the house and fence outwards and the rocket and clouds outwards.

3. On the last spread, fold the outer planet outwards and the inner planet inwards.

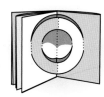

✏ USE IT!

- Tell a story using speech bubbles, with one character on the lefthand page and a different character on the righthand page.

- Make a story using pictures only. The pop-up shapes should help in planning the artwork.

- Fold the book inside out so that the story begins with a planet, then a rocket and finally a house. See what kind of stories the children can come up with.

Add more shapes

1. Follow the instructions to make the basic pop-up origami book, but make three pop-ups on each spread as shown.

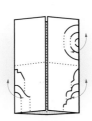

2. Fold the origami book. Open each spread and fold the pop-up shapes, folding some inwards and some outwards.

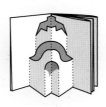

3. On the last spread, fold all the planet shapes outwards. Then fold the middle circle inwards and the last inner circle outwards.

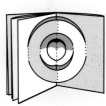

✏ USE IT!

- Make each pop-up a different house. Outline personal profiles of the characters.

- Ask the children to write instructions for making a basic pop-up origami book, using captions and diagrams. Make it into a zigzag book.

- Ask the children to photocopy their finished books and cut them out and fold to give to friends with personal messages written on the covers.

4 – Amazing storybooks

This is a landscape version of the basic origami book on page 6 and is ideal for pupils to make into an illustrated storybook for younger children. Experiment with folding the cover into a picture design. Some pages of the book lift or drop as well as turn.

Make the basic kite book

1. Open an A3 zigzag book (page 6) and cut in three places as shown.

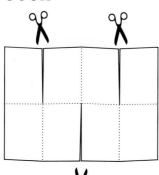

2. Fold the top middle panels down towards you.

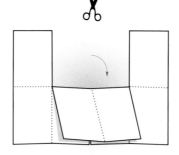

3. Fold the outer panels outwards, towards the back of the middle panels.

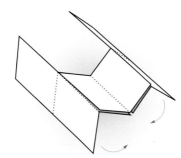

4. Fold the top panels down.

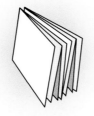

5. Turn sideways, so book is landscape.

6. Find the page with the crease at the bottom. This will be the kite.

7. Fold the bottom of this panel diagonally upwards to form a triangle shape. Fold the top two edges inwards along the dotted lines shown, to form a kite shape. Glue the kite to the front and back cover.

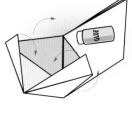

✏ USE IT!

- Discuss different issues with the children, such as how laws affect us and write a storybook to cover these issues. The story could describe a character that tries to rescue a kite from an electricity pylon.

- Compare an Edwardian beach holiday with a holiday of today. The cover shape could be used as a kite or an ice cream cone.

Magic star book

1. Follow the instructions for the basic kite book up to step 5. Fold the base of the crease upwards to form a triangle shape. Cut off the extra top edge.

2. Open the triangle shape and fold in half diagonally.

3. Push the crease upwards again to form the triangle shape. Open the triangle a little and tuck the top triangles inside, to form a diamond shape.

4. Cut out four small triangles from the sides of the diamond as shown, to form a star shape and glue down to the front and back of the book.

Hidden pages book

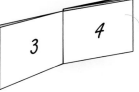

1. Follow the instructions for the basic kite book up to step 5.
Number the insides pages 1, 2, 3, 4. Find page 4 and fold down towards you.

2. These are the hidden pages. Number the top page 5, and the bottom page 6. Fold back to page 4 and continue numbering the pages (7, 8, 9, 10).

✏ USE IT!

• Write a story about a star that comes to Earth. What does it find strange about our planet?

• Put together a book of 'stars'. Can include sports personalities, film stars or those who have done something special to help others.

✏ USE IT!

• Plan a story around the hidden pages. Reveal a picture of a haunted house or a secret message on the hidden pages and continue the story.

• Write a story about a shipwreck. Put a map of a tropical island on the hidden pages showing places that will feature in the story.

'The Talking Kite' by Saira (aged 9). This kite book is an example of the first suggestion in USE IT! It is a cautionary tale about not playing with kites near electricity pylons.

5 – Our world books

A circle can represent the Sun or the Earth, a pie chart, or even the face of an important historical figure. The pop-up circle is easy-to-make and lends itself to a range of ideas, making it immediately attractive to children.

Make the basic pop-up book

1. Open an A3 zigzag book (page 6). Unfold. Fold in half widthways. On the folded edge, cut a quarter circle along to the horizontal crease as shown. Fold the quarter circle down over the bottom panel at a slight angle. Fold backwards and unfold.

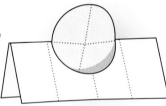

2. Open sheet. Fold top half behind bottom half, lengthways.

3. Fold in half widthways. At the same time, fold the pop-up inwards on the creased angle, so that it folds inside the book.

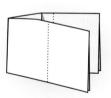

✎ USE IT!

- Make book about of the Earth's food production using the pop-up circle as a pie chart. Use the reverse side if more space is needed.

- Use the pop-up circle book to illustrate the Sun and the planets in our solar system. Discuss what information and key points should be included.

- Retell the story of King Arthur, using the pop-up as the centrepiece.

Our planet

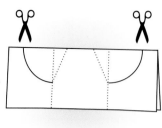

1. Fold an A3 sheet of paper in half lengthways. Fold widthways in three equal parts (page 5). Unfold. Cut two quarter circles as shown.

2. Fold both quarter circles forwards at a slight angle over the middle panel. Fold backwards and unfold.

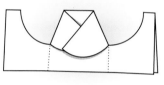

3. Open sheet. Fold the left and right panels back over the middle panel. Lift up the pop-up semi circles.

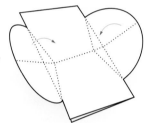

4. Fold in half widthways so the semi-circles overlap.

✎ USE IT!

- Draw the world on the pop-up, indicating where the richest and poorest people live. Outline the facts on the back.

- Draw Europe, the Atlantic and North and South America on the pop-up and show the journey that Columbus made to America on his third visit.

- Make a brochure advertising a luxury cruise. Show the countries visited on the map and use bullet points to describe four special events taking place during the cruise.

Homes and villages

1. Fold an A4 sheet of paper in half lengthways. Fold angles on the folded edge as shown. The bottom fold is at a lesser angle than the top one. Unfold and fold backwards. Cut off the extra paper overlapping the rest of the sheet.

2. Open sheet and tuck in the sides as you fold along the main centre crease.

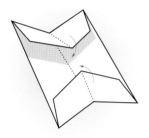 

USE IT!

- Make a book about family. Draw your family on the top panel, your home on the bottom panel and use the middle panel to list things that you are grateful for.

- Compare villages and cities. Draw a village on the top panel and skyscrapers on the bottom panel and use the middle panel to compare the two environments.

- Think about children in villages in India. Draw a village in India on the top panel, children working in fields on the bottom panel and use the middle panel to write a diary entry for one of the children.

'The World's Produce' by Jessica (aged 8). This pop-up book project took two afternoons. The text focuses on farming in different continents. The border includes food from these continents while also decorating the page.

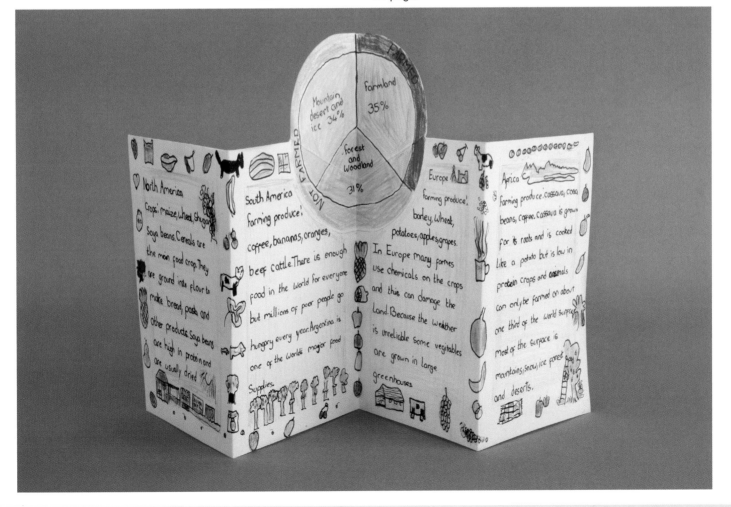

19

6 – Decorative spine books

This attractive 12-page book is made solely from cutting and folding a sheet of paper. As it folds into 16 panels, it's best to start with a large sheet of paper. The unusual spinal design is an integral part of the book.

Make the basic flag book

1. Open an A2 zigzag book (page 6). Fold the top and bottom edges to the centre. Unfold. Fold in half widthways and cut as shown. Unfold.

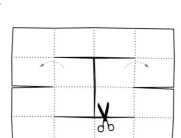

2. Cut the central crease of the middle panels.

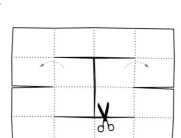

3. Open the middle panels.

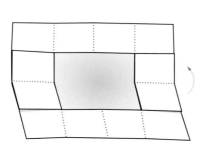

4. Fold the bottom half over the top half.

5. Fold the front top panels down. Do the same to the other side. Take both ends and push towards the centre to make a cube.

6. Push further to make a cross shape.

7. Fold the pages together as shown.

8. Roll the spine around a pencil and glue in place so that you have a tube shape.

9. Glue a flag into the tube spine.

✏ USE IT!

- Make an imaginary holiday diary, dividing each page into morning, afternoon and evening.

- Make a European country guidebook. Include traditions, climate, food, sport and useful phrases and illustrate with drawings.

- Make a book about WWII. Put a Union Jack in the spine. Describe different aspects of the war, such as home life, air raids, diet and ration books.

⭐ Helpful hint: It will be easier to write and draw in the book before the tube spine (step 8) has been completed.

Tepee book

1. Follow the instructions for the basic flag book up to step 7. Fold the cover in half widthways and then in half again. Unfold.

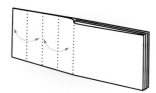

2. Fold the cover into four sections using the creases you have made as shown. Glue together on the inside.

3. Use the book in the portrait position to resemble a tepee.

✎ USE IT!

• Make a book about Native American Indians. Include sections on how they travelled, their clothes and how to make a model tepee.

• Retell an aboriginal or Native American story in six parts. Use the rich visual imagery of these cultures in the illustrations.

• Make a reporter's notebook. Write down the observations of an imaginary journalist covering an important event, such as a marathon or severe weather conditions.

Victorian book

1. Follow the instructions for the basic flag book up to step 7. Fold the cover in half widthways. Unfold and open into a box shape. Tie cotton around the spine to hold the pages in place.

✎ USE IT!

• Make a book about school in Victorian times. Write about discipline, lessons and clothes. Use the cover to make a model of a school.

• Describe a Victorian workhouse. Cover a different topic on each page, using the first page as the contents page, the second as an introduction and summarise on the last page.

• Make a book about a British king or queen. Draw a timeline along the top of all the pages and record key dates. Use the cover to make a model of the king or queen's palace.

'Italy' by George (aged 9). George has used the flag design to create a visitor's guide to Italy, including information about famous buildings, transport, food and useful phrases.

7 – Map fold books

The map fold is an ideal way of reducing plans and diagrams to a manageable size. It is also a smart way of presenting information. Grid referencing introduces an alternative to page numbering.

Make the basic fold-down map

1. Fold an A3 sheet of paper in half widthways. Fold in half widthways again. Unfold. Fold into three equal horizontal parts. Unfold. Fold the top four panels backwards and the bottom four panels forwards.

2. Fold into a zigzag.

TITLE

✏️ USE IT!

- Draw and narrate the journey of a traditional story character, such as 'Little Red Riding Hood'. Start at the top left page and finish at the bottom right page.

- Make a map of your neighbourhood. Using the creases in the paper as a grid draw places of interest such as the park, sports centre, cinema, etc. Number the grid down the left and right sides and add letters along the top and bottom. Use the last bottom panel as a contents page.

- Make a treasure hunt board game. Write instructions on the panels to make the players go forwards or backwards. Use dice and counters.

⭐ Helpful hint: For some projects, it may be better to fold the paper after the text and illustrations have been completed.

Pop-out map

1. Fold paper in half lengthways. Unfold. Fold in half widthways. Turn the paper so that the fold is at the top and fold the corners down to the vertical centre crease. Fold backwards. Unfold.

2. Tuck the left and right corners inwards.

3. Fold the front left edge to the middle crease. Unfold and fold backwards. Unfold. Do the same to other three sides.

4. Take the front left panel and push along the crease to fold it inwards. Do the same to the other three panels.

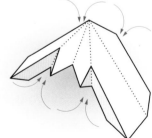

5. Turn it over to open the pop-out map.

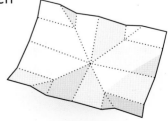

✏️ USE IT!

- Ask the class to design an adventure playground for the school. Illustrate and label a map of the site.

- Continue the story of the 'Three Little Pigs' after the ending of the traditional story. Create a map to show the adventure.

- Make a dental hygiene instruction leaflet, using the inside of the map as a mouth.

Locked map card

1. Fold an A3 sheet of paper in half lengthways. Unfold. Fold the top and bottom edges towards the centre crease lengthways. Cut a 1 cm slot in the centre of the left and right edges.

2. Interlock the slots to make a cylinder shape.

3. Press down to make the card.

✏️ USE IT!

- Make a party invitation. Design an attractive cover. Write the party details (date, time, place) on the inside panel. The outer panels can be used to advertise party games and party food.

- Make a leaflet advertising dog-walking services. Ask the children to think about what activities they could offer to make themselves sound attractive.

- Think about reducing energy in the home. Use the nine inside panels to write about different ways of achieving this.

'Our playground' by Julie (aged 7). This is an example of the first suggestion for the pop-up map in USE IT! Julie used a printout from a playground equipment website to help her plan a new playground for her school.

8 – Never-ending books

This is ideal for a medium to long-term project. The book can extend to any number of pages by joining zigzag page sections and making a cover. The children can also attach leaflets, mounted work, pockets and sleeves to hold additional information.

Make the basic never-ending book

1. For the book pages: use 4 sheets of A4 paper. Fold paper in half to make A5. Join each piece of paper with masking tape at the back along the edge.

2. For the cover: using A3 paper lengthways measure 2 cm from the right edge. Fold the left edge to this measurement. Unfold and do the same to the other side. This makes a 2 cm spine. If there are more than 10 pages or there is mounted work on the pages, add another centimetre to the side measurements to increase the width of the spine.

3. Open the cover and place the pages inside (with one page open). Fold top and bottom edges of the cover over the pages. Remove the pages and sharpen the creases. Unfold.

4. Place pages (with pages closed) inside the open cover, with the right edge touching the left side of the spine. Fold the left 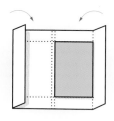 edge of the cover over the pages. Remove the pages and sharpen the crease. Repeat this to the right side.

5. Turn the cover over. Fold each corner diagonally where the vertical and horizontal creases meet. Unfold.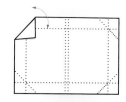

6. Turn the cover over. Fold the left and top edges over where you made the folds earlier. At the same time, use the diagonal crease you made on the corner, so that you make a square shape on the corner. Do the same to the other sides and corners.

7. Tuck the first and last pages of the book into the corners.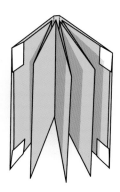

> ★ Helpful tip: You can strengthen the cover with card on the inside.

Folded leaflet

1. Fold an A4 sheet of paper in half widthways and then in half again widthways. This is your leaflet. Glue the back to a page in the book.

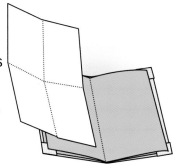

Picture mounts

1. Fold an A8 sheet of paper diagonally to cover the biggest area possible. Cut off the extra bit of paper. Unfold. This will leave you with a square. Fold diagonally in the opposite direction. Unfold. Cut away one triangle shape from the square. Fold one triangle towards you, along the diagonal crease. Do the same with the last triangle, gluing it on top of the other one, to make the picture mount.

2. Make another mount in the same way. Tuck opposite corners of any work to be mounted as shown and glue the back of the mounts to the page.

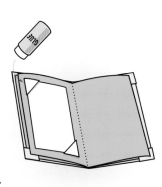

✏ USE IT!

- Ask the children to think about how they can use leaflets and mounts to add extra information to their projects without having to add more pages. The leaflet could be used to attach magazine or newspaper articles. Mounts ensure that photos can be easily removed. They can be made with decorative paper.

Pocket

1. Using A5 paper, fold each side over a ruler width. Unfold and cut off 2 of the corners diagonally at the point where the horizontal and vertical creases meet.

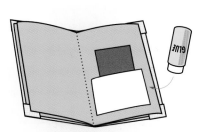

2. Fold the 4 sides along the creases and glue 3 of the sides to the page.

✏ USE IT!

- The pocket can be used for storing additional information and labels, tickets, newspaper cuttings. Don't store too much in it though. Make another pocket if necessary.

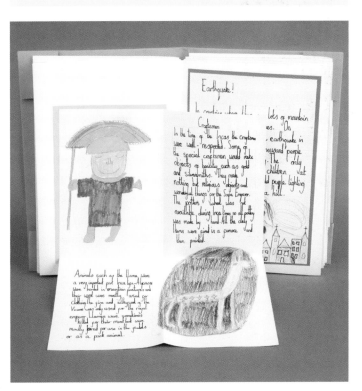

'South America' by Rebecca (aged 11). This project extended over several weeks and covered geographical, environmental, cultural and social aspects of the South American continent, using several presentation methods and writing styles.

9 – Spine lock books

This is a good book for a short-term project. The folded pattern on the spine is very attractive especially if coloured paper is used and it also keeps the pages in place. The children can experiment with diagonal and horizontal creases to make their own variations.

Make the basic central diamond lock

1. Put 2 sheets of A4 paper together. Fold in half widthways. On the folded edge, find the centre and measure 1 cm either side of this and measure 1 cm horizontally from these measurements. Measure another 2 cm up from the top measurement and 2 cm down from the bottom measurement. Cut diagonally from the 2 cm measurements to the 1 cm measurement as shown.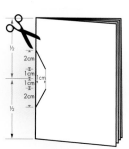

2. Open the sheets of paper with the creased edge facing you. Fold the top triangle shape down and the bottom triangle up over it.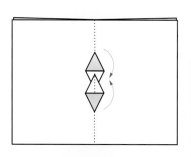

3. Fold the sheets of paper in half again to make the closed book.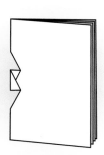

✏️ USE IT!

- Plan a party menu. Page 1 could list drinks, page 2 sandwiches and so on.

- Make a book about musical instruments. Describe how you make sounds with the instruments.

- Make a book of mosaic and non-mosaic patterns.

- Ask the children to make a record of their achievements, listing different school subjects on each page.

Top and bottom diamonds

1. Follow the instructions for the central diamond lock, but move the measurements and diagonal cuts further apart, so that you have 2 separate locks.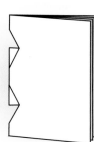

✏️ USE IT!

- Ask the class to think about how many hours they spend in school, outdoor activities, eating, sleeping, etc each week and use bar charts to record their results.

- Ask the class to think about favourite things. Use the title 'Why I like…' and use the book to complete this thought and write about hobbies, sports, places and people.

- Plan a holiday, including information about essential things to take, dangers you might come across and how to ensure that the holiday is a success.

Square corners

1. Put 2 sheets of A4 paper together. Fold in half widthways. On the folded edge, measure 2 cm down from the top and 2 cm horizontally from the fold. Mark out a square on this corner using these measurements. Cut away the remaining rectangle of paper at the top of the paper. Do the same at the bottom of the paper.

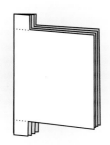

Below: 'Highlights of My Holiday' in France by Craig (aged 8). Craig has made a feature of his square corners by decorating them with the French flag.

Below right: 'Kids' Party Menu' by Bethany (aged 7). This is an example of the first suggestion from USE IT! for the central diamond lock book. Bethany has listed food and drinks under headings such as Starters and Main Meals on each page.

2. Open the sheets of paper with the creased edge facing you. Fold the top rectangle shape down and the bottom rectangle up.

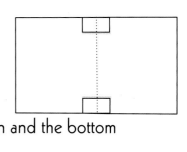

3. Fold the sheets of paper in half again to make the closed book.

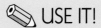 USE IT!

- Ask the class to write down their rights and responsibilities. Write down rights on the left-hand pages and responsibilities on the right-hand pages.

- Make a book entitled 'How to be Happy'. Describe a different way of finding happiness on each page.

- Make a scrapbook of family photos. Include captions for each photo and write something interesting about each person.

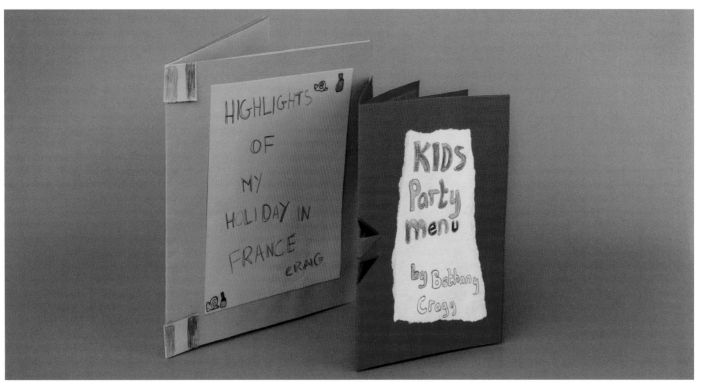

10 – Compilation books *and Computer*

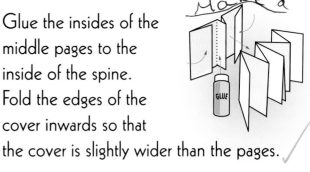

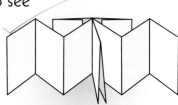

The middle pages, rather than the first and last pages, of these books are glued or stitched into the cover. These means the pages can be spread out in both directions from the centre and also that individual sheets of work or smaller books can be attached to the cover.

Make the basic panorama book

1. For the pages, open an A3 zigzag book (page 6). Cut along the middle crease (lengthways), leaving the last panel uncut. Fold in half lengthways. Zigzag the top sheet along the creases and then the back sheet, so that it looks like this with an upside-down V-shaped piece in the middle as shown.

2. For the cover, fold an A3 sheet of paper in half lengthways. Then fold in half widthways. Measure 3 cm across from the folded edge and fold along this measurement. Unfold and fold backwards. Unfold.

3. Tuck the fold along the spine inwards, to form an 'M' shape.

4. Glue the insides of the middle pages to the inside of the spine. Fold the edges of the cover inwards so that the cover is slightly wider than the pages.

5. Open the pages to see the finished book.

✏ USE IT!

- Make a book about a famous river, such as the Amazon or the Thames. Or, draw different types of shoreline and explain the effects of erosion and climate change.

- Compare different types of habitat – the left-hand pages can deal with hot climates and the right-hand pages can deal with hot ones.

- Make a book about rainforests before and after deforestation. The left-hand pages can show the rainforest in bloom and the right-hand pages can show it after deforestation.

Three sections book

1. Cut A3 paper in half lengthways. Take one piece and fold in half widthways. Fold in half again widthways and unfold. Fold the folded edge to the centre crease. Unfold.

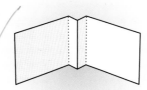

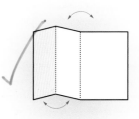

2. Leaving the first and last panels, fold each of the middle panels in half to make a zigzag. This is the cover.

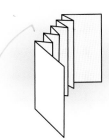

3. Fold 3 A5 sheets of paper in half widthways and glue to the insides of the zigzags.

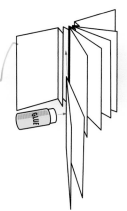

---

2. Inside the cover, zigzag the creases of the spine.

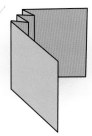

3. For the pages, cut an A4 sheet of paper in half widthways. Put the 2 pieces together and fold in half widthways. Make 2 equally spaced holes on the fold. Sew the pages through the first zigzag fold inside the cover. Tie a knot on the inside and trim the cotton. Create another set of pages and join to the second zigzag fold.

4. Open the pages to see the finished book and trim down the cover to the edge of the pages.

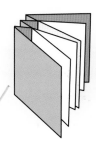

✏ USE IT!

- Ask the children to put together information, including dates of birth, height, food preferences, about the other children in the class.

- Ask the class to think about their local environment. Illustrate and label ways of improving it.

- Make a book of art. Draw three pieces of artwork inspired by a famous artist, and include interesting information about the artist.

⭐ Helpful hint: Complete the writing before gluing the pages into the cover.

Stitched book

1. For the cover, fold an A3 sheet of paper in half lengthways. Fold in half widthways. Measure 3 cm across from the folded edge and fold along this measurement. Unfold. Fold backwards and unfold. Fold the folded edge to the 3 cm measurement. Unfold. Fold backwards and unfold.

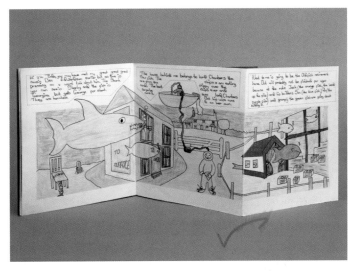

'Life above and below water' by Lou (aged 12). This is an original story about a community on dry land and another one underwater. The elongated illustrations are ideal for this book.

11 – Triangle books

These three triangular-shaped books are all different. Triangle books are popular with children because of their unusual structure and it can also be fun to fit words into the varying line lengths.

Make the basic triangle book

1. Fold an A3 sheet of paper diagonally from the top left corner to cover the biggest area possible. Unfold. Fold another diagonal from the bottom left corner. Unfold. Fold in half lengthways. Unfold. Fold vertically where the diagonal creases meet and fold the remaining rectangle of paper over. Cut square as shown.

2. Starting with the bottom right triangle, fold along the creases, alternating between folding over and under. Wrap the rectangle panel around the triangles to make a cover. Fold the rectangle behind the triangle and then fold the remaining piece over the other side of the triangle to make the cover.

3. Tuck the corners in and glue down lightly.

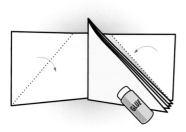
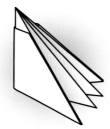

✏️ USE IT!

- Make a book of spells. On the left-hand pages write down ingredients for the spells and write down or draw the results of the spells on the right-hand pages.

- Make a book about mountains. Use the mountain shape of the book to write about three famous mountains in the world.

- Continue the 'Pied Piper of Hamelin' story. Write an outline of the story on the first two spreads. Continue the story on the last spread describing how the children escaped from the mountain and return to their village.

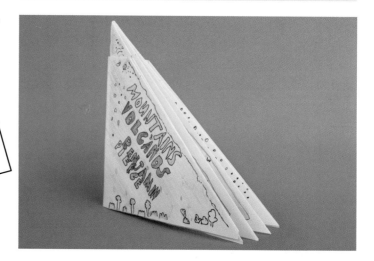

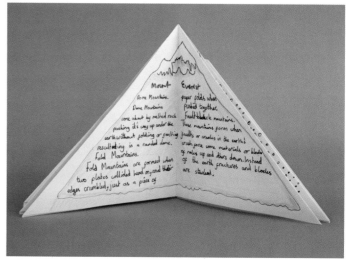

'Mountains and Volcanoes' by Benjamin (aged 11). Benjamin uses the triangular-shaped pages to enhance his subject.

Pyramid book

1. Fold an A3 sheet of paper in half lengthways. Fold into three equal 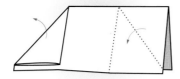 vertical parts (page 6) and unfold. Fold the top left corner diagonally forwards and unfold. Do the same to the right side.

2. Open the edge of the left corner and tuck inwards. Do the same to the right side. Fold 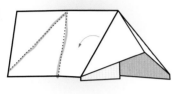 the right triangles over the middle panel and fold the left triangles over this.

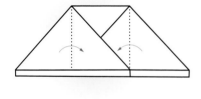

Triangle book with square pages

1. Cut out the largest square possible from A3 paper. Fold in half horizontally. Unfold. Fold in half vertically. Unfold. Fold in half diagonally in both directions and unfold.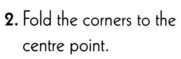

2. Fold the corners to the centre point.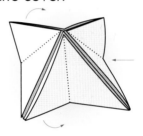

3. Fold the other triangles inwards to make 3 spreads and close the last triangle to make the cover.

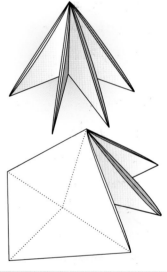

4. Fold down the pages/ flaps on each triangle to make square pages.

✏️ USE IT!

- Think about the Indus Valley civilisation and write about a different aspect of the civilisation on each triangle.

- Ask the class to think about how ancient Egyptians constructed pyramids. Number the pages and describe the process stage-by-stage on each page.

- Write a circus story about animals that refuse to perform. Explain the story on the left-side spread and the solution on the right-side spread. Draw the big top in the main area and use the outer triangle for the title and author's name.

✏️ USE IT!

- Write a book about religion. Write the title of a different religious festival, e.g. Divali (Hinduism), Eid (Islam) and Easter (Christianity) on the three spreads. Open the pages and write about how these festivals are celebrated.

- Write a book about ghosts, for example Shakespeare's Macbeth, or use the spreads to write about the three ghosts in 'A Christmas Carol' by Charles Dickens.

- Make a book of riddles. Write a riddle on top of the flap and the answer underneath.

12 – Slot books

One of the problems with cutting and lifting a panel for 3D artwork is that it creates a gap. The advantage of these books is that they use a slotting device so that the page stays intact. The technique can be used in many ways.

Make the basic slot book

1. Fold A3 sheet of paper in half lengthways and widthways and unfold. With the paper lengthways, fold the left and right edges to the centre crease. In the top panels, cut the shape of a building or artefact along the folded edges. Make sure you don't cut through the whole shape.

2. Fold the bottom half of the paper behind the top half. Fold the shapes that you have cut out forwards. Cut the paper behind this half in line with the fold of your shapes. Flatten your shapes and unfold the whole sheet.

3. Fold widthways and push the shapes through the slots. Fold in half widthways to make the book.

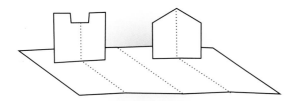

✏️ USE IT!

- Make a travel brochure. Make the cut-out shapes into famous buildings, such as the Eiffel Tower and the Taj Mahal. Write text to advertise the buildings.

- Construct a Viking or Roman settlement. Ask the children to think about why these people invaded Britain.

- Ask the children to think about religious symbols. Make the cut-out shapes a mosque and a synagogue and write about how we can identify a religion by the symbols.

Two-layer slot book

1. Fold a sheet of A3 paper in half lengthways. Unfold and fold in half widthways. With the folded edge on the left, cut a house shape in the top half as shown.

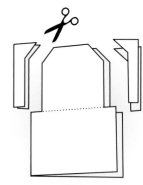

2. Fold in half widthways and cut a vertical slot just below the crease, from the folded edge to the width of the house. Unfold the vertical crease.

3. Push the house shape through the slot.

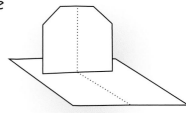

- Draw a medieval castle on the outer house shape and a diagram of the interior on the under panel. Ask the children to think about why castles were built and who lived in them.

- Compare the lives of rich and poor Victorian children. Draw the rich child's house on the outer shape and the poor child's house on the under shape. Begin each section with 'My name is…'.

Calendar book

1. Open an A3 zigzag book (page 6). Fold in half widthways. Measure 2 cm in from the edges and creases and cut 3 panels as shown, using these measurements.

2. Fold the left panel in half towards you. Measure 2 cm up from the middle crease and cut a slot from the folded edge to the width of the cut shape beneath it. Unfold.

3. Fold in half widthways and push all flaps through the slot.

4. Turn over and stand up like a desktop calendar.

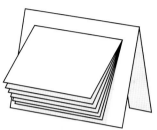

- Write down important dates, such as St Valentine's Day and Armistice on each page.

- Make Florence Nightingale's diary. Imagine her working day among the wounded during the Crimean.

'The Romans' by Amelia (aged 10). Amelia's slot book, describing Roman villas and baths, is the centrepiece, but she has extended the project with a pop-up, instruction manual and promotional leaflet.

13 – Hinged pop-ups

A ninety-degree pop-up is one that opens to a ninety-degree angle (e.g. the pop-up origami book on page 14). These pop-ups usually cease vertically in the middle, but diagonal creases produce very different pop-ups.

Make the basic robot book

1. Fold an A4 sheet of paper in half widthways. On the unfolded edge, cut a robot head shape as shown. Fold the head forwards and backwards at an angle.

2. Open the sheet and fold the head inwards along the creases. Close paper and open to make the head pop up.

USE IT!

- Write an advertisement for a domestic robot. What makes it indispensable in the home?

- Ask the class to imagine that they are robot pupils. Ask them to write a letter to apply for a job. What makes them suitable for the job? Make the robot head into a self-portrait.

- Write an introduction to a science fiction story, describing the strengths and weaknesses of the main character, the robot.

Jumping animals

1. Fold an A4 sheet of paper in half widthways. Unfold. Fold in half lengthways. On the folded edge, cut halfway across the horizontal crease. On the folded edge, on the bottom panel, fold the corner diagonally forwards and backwards. Unfold. Make another diagonal fold in this triangle shape — fold it forwards and backwards. Unfold.

2. Open the sheet and fold in half vertically. Fold in half widthways so that the diagonal creases are on the inside. Pop the larger diagonal creases out. Fold the smaller diagonal creases inwards.

3. Fold an A6 sheet of paper in half lengthways. Unfold. Cut out a jumping animal, e.g. a monkey. Glue onto the pop out. Make sure that the animal pop-up doesn't stick out above the paper when closed.

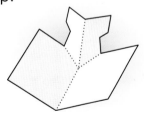

- Compare humans and animals. Write our similarities to a particular animal on one side and our differences on the other.

- Extend this project by making the pop-up the central spread of an origami book (page 14). Write a story about a captured animal being sold as a pet to Europe.

- Make a brochure to encourage people to support a monkey sanctuary.

Animals in hiding

1. Follow the instructions for step 1 for Jumping animals, but make 3 equally spaced diagonal folds. Fold each one forwards and backwards and unfold.

2. Open the sheet and fold in half vertically. Fold in half widthways so that the diagonal creases are on the inside. Pop the largest diagonal creases out. Fold the second diagonal creases in. Fold the last diagonal creases out.

3. Fold an A7 sheet of paper in half widthways. Unfold and cut as shown. Glue onto the back pop-up.

4. Fold a sheet of A7 paper in half widthways. Unfold and cut as shown. Glue onto the front pop-up.

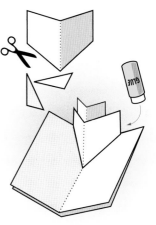

✏️ USE IT!

- Design a campaign to help protect an endangered animal. Draw the animal on the back pop-up and foliage on the front pop-up.

- What animal is hiding? Give clues to its identity beneath the pop-ups.

- Make a fact file on whales. Draw a whale on the back pop-up and waves on the front pop-up.

'Sharks' by Martha (aged 11). Rather than using a jumping animal, Martha's whale dives down into the sea. The journalistic-style text was adapted from a story in an Australian newspaper. Martha also put together a 'Save the Sharks' brochure.

14 – Bird pop-up book

This is a one hundred and eighty-degree pop-up book. The pop-up rises vertically on the horizontal page. In comparison to the ninety-degree pop-up, the pop-ups need to be glued in place. Ideas for the birds are given, but any birds can be used.

Make the basic owl pop-up

1. For the base, make an A3 origami book (page 6). For the pop-up, fold an A6 sheet of paper in half widthways. On the unfolded edge, cut an owl head as shown. At the bottom of the paper, fold the edge at an angle forwards and backwards.

2. Glue the owl along the folded edge and stick to the first spread of the origami book. Make sure that the central crease of the owl touches the central crease of the page.

- Make an information book about birds, describing their habitat and breeding habits.

- Ask the class to make an information book about birds, but using speech bubbles for the birds so that the birds can describe themselves.

- Write a book about how birds fly. Use each spread to cover a different aspect of the topic, e.g. the shape of the wings.

Sparrow

1. Follow the instructions for the owl pop-up, but make a sparrow's head on A6 paper. Note that the bird's head will not be symmetrical, as it will be drawn from a side view.

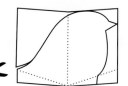

2. Glue the sparrow into the second spread of the book.

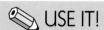

- Make a fact file about where and when to see certain birds in the UK. Are any species unusual in your own part of the country?

- Write an imaginary and fictional story about birds, where each bird thinks it is the king of birds and gives reasons for this.

Eagle

1. Follow the instructions for the sparrow pop-up, but make an eagle's head on A6 paper.

2. Glue the eagle into the third spread of the book.

- Make pop-ups of three different eagle species. Think about where they live, where they build their nests and include descriptions about their appearance and characteristics.

- Make a book about the eagle as a symbol of Native American or ancient Roman culture.

- Write a story about an owl, a sparrow and an eagle. Create tension in the narrative – are they in danger of losing their habitat? How are they saved?

'Parrots' by Rachael (aged 8). Rachael researched her subject on the Internet and in books from the school library to create this fact file.

15 – Pop-up Greek legends

The diagonal creases we used in the bird pop-up books take a new direction here. In this project, we'll use them to make a standing figure and a pop-up mountain.

The sea god

1. For the base, fold an A3 sheet of paper in half widthways and unfold.

2. For the pop-up, fold an A4 sheet of paper widthways into a 'W' zigzag. Crease 1 cm margin on the bottom edge. Cut away as shown.

3. Fold into a zigzag and fold the 2 tabbed edges on the bottom upwards. Glue the right tab to the inside of the base as shown. Glue the other edge and fold the base over it to stick.

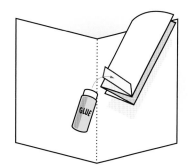

✏️ USE IT!

- Retell one of the stories about the sea god, Poseidon. Draw waves and sea creatures lightly on the base so that it can be used as a background for the text.

- Design a package holiday advertisement for a holiday complex called 'Poseidon'. Included a list of the facilities provided and an application form. Are there any discounts for children?

The gods of Mount Olympus

1. For the base, fold an A3 sheet of paper in half widthways. On the folded edge, make a diagonal fold to the centre of the top edge. Unfold. Make another diagonal fold in the corner. Unfold. Fold both creases backwards and unfold.

2. Open sheet and pop the back creases outwards and the front creases inwards.

3. For the mountain, fold an A4 sheet of paper in half widthways. Fold the bottom edge of the paper and unfold. On the folded edge, cut away a triangle. Cut out a mountain shape. Open the mountain and glue the tabbed edge to the back diagonal creases on the base.

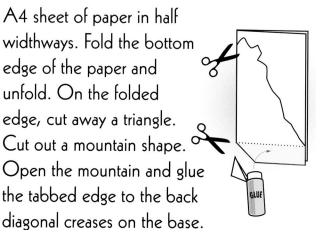

38

4. For the figures, fold an A6 sheet of paper in half lengthways. Make the folded edges at the bottom in the same way as the mountain. Make another figure. Glue their tabbed edges to the front diagonal creases on the base — do this at a right angle so half the edge is on the crease and half is on the flat paper.

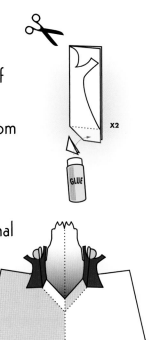

✏️ USE IT!

- Ask the class to put together a project about Apollo and Zeus using other techniques, such as picture mounts (page 25) to hold a drawing of a god or include a map of ancient Greece (page 22), as well as the techniques above.

- Update an Olympic god's story. What could replace a mountain? What would Zeus look like today? What is the contemporary equivalent of his thunderbolt?

'Zeus and Apollo' by Steven (aged 10). Steven has extended his project to include pockets and flaps. Information about the two gods is recorded using bullet points, while more detailed information is held in the pockets.

16 – Building through the ages

Pop-up buildings are straightforward to make and can add zest to historical projects. The basic construction can be adapted for other subjects too.

Tudor house

1. For the base, fold an A3 sheet of paper in half widthways. Unfold.

2. For the house, cut a sheet of A3 paper in half lengthways. Take one piece and make a fold on the right edge. Glue the left edge to this edge and fold flat.

3. Measure 1 cm up on the bottom edge and make a crease on this measurement. Unfold. Measure 3 cm across on the left and right edges and make creases on these measurements. Fold all creases backwards and forwards. Cut away the top and bottom as shown. Fold the top edge forwards along the crease.

★ Helpful tip: Join the finished pop-up building to the bases first, so that the children have something exciting in front of them to write about.

4. On the base, measure 3 cm up from the centre crease. Glue along the bottom edge of the house and stick to the base (with the top pointing away from the measurement). Make sure the crease of the house touches the measurement. Glue the other edge at the bottom of the house and fold the base over to stick.

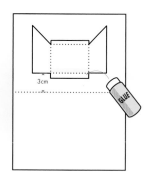
3cm

5. Open the base to see pop-up house.

6. For the roof, fold an A5 sheet of paper in half widthways. Fold the edges at the top of the house outwards and glue the roof to these edges.

✎ USE IT!

- Use a map fold book (page 22) to draw and caption important events of a particular historical period. Glue this to the base of the pop-up house. Use capital letters for the title on the front cover and write text on the back cover to advertise the project. It could begin with, 'In this pop-up Tudor house you will…'

- Make a fold down (page 22), showing the downstairs and upstairs plan of the house. Label the rooms and outline their uses. Glue this to the base of the house.

- Add diagrams around the pop-up house to show the stage-by-stage construction of a Tudor house.

Factory

1. Follow the instructions for the Tudor house to Stage 1, but use A4 paper at Stage 2. Fold in half vertically and open up into a box shape. Make another box in the same way.

2. Cut a 4 cm wide strip from the short edge of A5 paper. Fold in half lengthways and glue together to make the chimney. Glue both box shapes together with the chimney in the middle as shown.

3. Fold the factory flat, along the creases and glue the bottom of one of the boxes along the centre crease of the base. Apply glue to the bottom of the other box and fold the base over to stick.

Skyscraper

1. Make the base in the same way as the Tudor house base. Make a fold on the long edge of an A4 sheet of paper. Glue the other edge to this and fold flat. Fold in half lengthways and unfold.

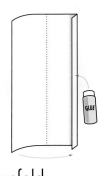

2. Fold the bottom edge and cut away as shown.

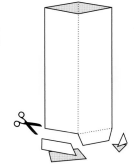

3. Glue the tabbed edge to the base on one side of the centre crease at a 45-degree angle as shown. Glue the other tabbed edge and fold the base over to stick. Cut away any paper that is visible outside of the folded base.

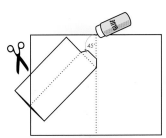

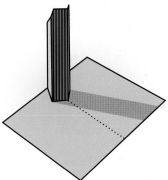

✎ USE IT!

- Ask the class to imagine that they are parents of children working in Victorian Britain and to write an account. Write this account in an origami book (page 6) and glue this to the base of the factory.

- Imagine this is a chocolate factory and that something has gone wrong in the manufactory process with devastating consequences. Make the story exciting and full of suspense.

✎ USE IT!

- Ask the class to think about what new building materials and techniques changed 20th century architecture. Write about how high-rise buildings changed people's lives.

- Discuss with the class how the lifestyle of people living in residential skyscrapers can be different to others. Using a Q & A interview technique, ask them to write an article about one family for a magazine around the pop-up.

17 – Fan pop-ups

Fans made from paper and mounted on bamboo have a long history that goes back to ancient China, although the folded variety is thought to have originated in Japan. Because fans zigzag down flat they lend themselves to pop-up book illustrations.

Chinese fan

1. For the base, fold an A4 sheet of paper in half widthways. Unfold. For the fan, cut an A4 sheet of paper in half lengthways. Take one piece and fold it in half widthways. Fold it in half again and unfold. Fold the left and right sides to the centre crease. Unfold and zigzag to form a 'W' shape. Fold an A7 sheet of paper in half lengthways and glue to the underside of the first zigzag panel. Do the same to the last zigzag panel.

2. Glue one side to the base as shown. Glue the top strip and fold the base over to stick.

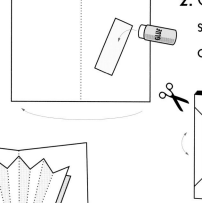

★ Helpful tip: Complete the artwork before making the fan.

✏️ USE IT!

- Some Chinese fans show scenes of everyday life. Discuss with the class what they could show on their fans, e.g. playing in a park, a football match, etc.

- On the front and back of the base, write a brief history of the Chinese fan, using the internet to research the subject.

Zigzag pop-up

1. For the base, fold an A3 sheet of paper in half widthways. Unfold. For the pop-up, cut away 4 cm from the long edge of a sheet of A3 paper. Fold in the same way as step 1 for the fan. With the folded paper in the 'M' position, make 2 cuts in the paper as shown on each of the 4 folded edges. Fold the inner sections that you've just made forwards and backwards and unfold. Turn the paper to the 'W' position and pop out the inner sections.

2. Glue the back of the last panel to the base as shown. Glue the first panel and fold the base over to stick.

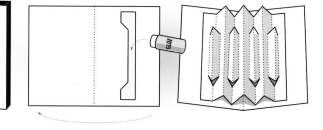

★ Helpful tip: Older children with good quality scissors will be able to cut through the four inner fold pop-ups at once. Younger children should cut them individually.

- This is a street scene from the 1940s. Use arrows to explain why the houses have stick paper over the windows. Include a poster of the period like 'Dangerous talk costs lives' on the wall.

- Before folding the zigzag, draw a snake wriggling across it. Use the internet to look at snake stories from around the world. Choose one of the stories and retell the story in your own words. Begin the narrative beneath the pop-up and continue on the back.

Water bird

1. For the base, fold an A4 sheet of paper in half widthways. Unfold. For the bird's body, fold an A4 sheet of paper in half widthways. Fold in half again and unfold. Fold left and right sides to the centre crease. Unfold and zigzag the panels to the 'W' position. Unfold and fold in half lengthways. Unfold. Cut along this crease, leaving the last panel uncut.

2. Zigzag the top half and glue the last panel to the last panel of the bottom half. Zigzag the bottom half. Apply glue to the edge of the panel as shown.

3. Glue to base as shown. Apply glue to the top panel in the same place as the bottom panel and fold the base over to stick.

4. For the neck and head, cut a sheet of A6 paper in half lengthways. Take one piece and fold as shown to make the bird's head. Make the same folds to both sides of the paper.

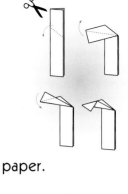

5. Glue the neck to the front of the fan folds. Add a drop of glue to the 2 sides of the beak to keep them together if needed.

✏️ USE IT!

- Imagine this is the final spread from 'The Ugly Duckling' pop-up book. Around the pop-up, write down the final episode in your own words.

- Design a poster for animal aid. Explain and write down the dangers of throwing rubbish, such as cans and polythene bags, into the habitats of water birds around your pop-up.

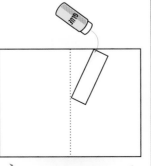

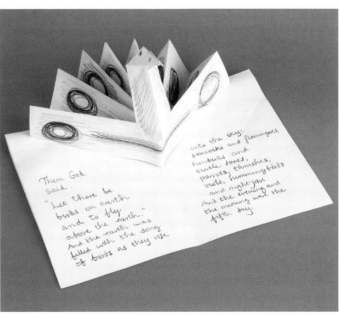

'Then God said...' by Jason (aged 12). This is a spread from a pop-up book on Bible stories.

18 — Pop-up windows

This pop-up can be put on a wall like a picture. Unlike most pop-ups it is quite shallow and so takes up very little space. It makes a great toy theatre and I remember having a nativity in this style as a child in the 1950s. However, it has many variations.

Make the basic presentation frame

1. For the base, fold an A4 sheet of paper in half widthways and unfold. For the frame, measure 1 cm, then 2 cm, then 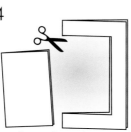 1 cm from the short edge of an A4 sheet of paper. Cut along the 4 cm measure and lightly score the other markings on this strip. Fold the rest of the paper in half widthways and cut away a window on the folded edge as shown.

2. Cut the strip into 4 equal pieces.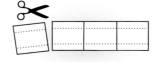

3. Take 1 piece and fold in half widthways. Cut the top and bottom as shown.

4. Fold the creases at the top and bottom. Glue the middle panel together to make a bracket. Repeat step 3 to the other 3 pieces.

5. Glue 2 brackets to the window frame as shown.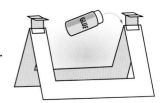

6. Glue these brackets to the centre of the base.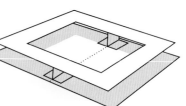

7. Fold frame in half, so that it's flat on right side of base. Glue bracket to the underside of the frame. Apply glue to the folded edge at the bottom of the bracket and fold base over the frame to stick. Open frame and repeat to the other side.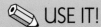

✏ USE IT!

- Make a frame for yourself to present the children's handwriting or artwork. You can change the work easily by using non-permanent adhesive.

- Make a seasonal collage picture on the piece of paper cut out from the centre of the frame and glue into the window area. Write a poem or reflective prose starting with 'What I like about…' around the edges of the frame before putting it together.

- Make a Christmas card – draw the nativity scene in the centre and write the words of your favourite carol around the frame.

Pop-up theatre with scenery

1. Make base in the same way as the presentation frame base. Using A4 paper, measure 1 cm and 2 cm from the left edge and fold along these measurements. Repeat to the right edge. Fold paper in half widthways. Cut away a window on the folded edge as shown.

2. The scenery is the same width as the frame (not including the folded edges). Measure 1 cm from the left and right edges and fold along these measurements. Fold in half widthways. Cut along the top to make your scene.

3. For the brackets, measure 1 cm, then 2 cm, then 1 cm from the short edge of the spare paper. Follow steps 2–5 for the frame above, but only make 2 brackets. Put the scenery inside the frame as shown with the folded edge folded outwards.

4. Glue the folded edge of the scenery to the folded edge of the frame. The scenery folded edge should be glued about half way across the frame folded edge. Repeat to the other side. Glue the brackets to the base.

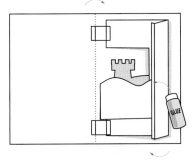

Apply glue to the 1 cm frame edge and fold the base over to stick. Repeat to the other side.

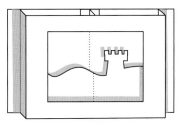

✏️ USE IT!

- Draw a favourite scene from a book you are reading on the scenery and backdrop. On the back of the theatre retell that scene. What did you find so captivating about it?

- Draw a famous building e.g. the Houses of Parliament, on the scenery. Underneath the frame, give reasons for visiting it. On the top part of the frame write, 'Don't miss visiting…'

⭐ Helpful tip: You don't have to draw right to the edge of the scenery, as part of it will be hidden by the frame.

'Noah's Ark' by Bethany (aged 10). The ark is the structural centrepiece of this pop-up theatre. Cut-out animals and Mr and Mrs Noah were glued to the ark. The retelling of the story is contained in a separate zigzag book.

19 – Story theatres

These theatres fascinated children in the 19th century and do so for today's children too. You might want to experiment with figures on strips of card (rod puppets) to act out a story or play. Wherever possible encourage the children to modify the design to make it their own.

Make the basic theatre book

1. Open an A3 zigzag book (page 6). Fold in half lengthways and then lengthways again. On the folded edge, cut a window from the second panel.

2. Open the sheet and cut as shown.

3. Fold in half lengthways and tuck the end panel with the flap into the other end, making sure that the other flap is on the outside.

4. Make and glue figures onto the base of theatre. The text can be written on the back pages.

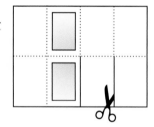
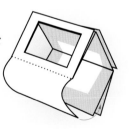

✏️ USE IT!

- Glue the figure of Aladdin holding his lamp and the genie into the theatre. On the back pages, write a scene from Aladdin in dialogue form.

- Make a Punch and Judy theatre. Outline the plot and characters and describe a typical Victorian beach scene.

- Looking into the future, make an imaginary scene of what the school playground will look like in 100 years time. Write about the kind of activities and equipment you would put there.

Standing theatre

1. Cut a thick A4 sheet of paper in half lengthways. On one piece, measure 1 cm from the left edge and crease. Measure another 4 cm from the crease and make another crease. Repeat to the other side. Cut four thin slots in between the creases as shown.

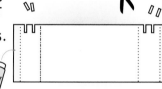

2. Fold along the creases and glue the edges to a sheet of A4 paper.

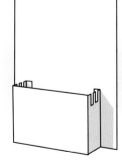

3. Make background scenery to slot into the stand.

- Make a rainforest picture, including trees, plants and animals to slot into the stand. Write about what we can do to save them on the front of the stand.

- Make a 3D picture of the Great Fire of London with smoke and fire on the back sheet and buildings in the slots. Record the progress of the fire in a zigzag book (page 6) and attach it to the stand.

- Make waves to put in the front slots and a mermaid to put in the back slots. On the front of the stand, describe what the mermaid is carrying in her purse. Ask the class to imagine the theatre is in a toy shop – what can they write on the back of the stand to make it appealing to customers?

Locking theatre

1. Photocopy the template on page 63. Lay the paper on a cutting mat or thick cardboard and cut the solid lines with a knife. Crease the dotted lines so that the middle sections fold into the centre. Interlock the top and bottom sections. Open the theatre by pulling the edges outwards.

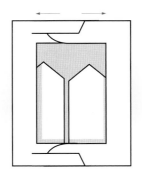

2. Close the theatre by pushing the edges inwards.

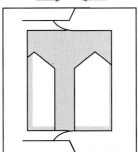

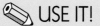

- Fill the theatre with acrobats and clowns and write a party invitation on the outer frame. Plan carefully what information you want to communicate.

- Include a coconut shy and a carousel in your fairground scene. List the attractions around the frame and add captions to make them sound attractive!

- Make a birthday card. Draw a party scene or the contents of a birthday present. Discuss with the class a one-sentence greeting. How witty can they make it?

'Victorian Fairground' by Amy (aged 7). Amy did the artwork on the opened flat theatre, but regularly closed it to see how it would appear when locked together. This way she avoided drawing intricate artwork in areas hidden from view.

20 – Paper mechanics

Push and pull slides are widely used in fiction and non-fiction children's books and in a variety of different ways. Capture the imagination of the class with these easy-to-make movables.

Before and after

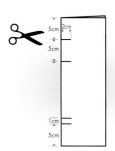

1. Fold an A4 sheet of paper in half lengthways. Cut slots as shown. Unfold.

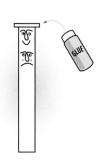

2. Cut a strip of thick paper 4 cm wide from the long edge of A4 paper. Glue a small piece of paper to the top of the strip.

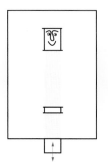

3. Weave the strip into the slots, putting it into the top slot first. Pull the strip down and draw a 'before' picture. Push the strip up and draw an 'after' picture.

✏️ USE IT!

- Draw a happy face at the top of the strip and a sad face lower down. On the left side of the sheet write what makes you happy and on the right side what makes you sad.

- Ask the class to think about healthy and unhealthy food. Draw a plate of unhealthy food as the 'before' picture at the top of the strip and healthy food lower down. Write a warning at the top of the sheet and comment on what makes a balanced diet.

Journeys

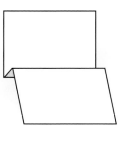

1. Fold an A4 sheet of paper in half widthways. With the folded edge at the bottom, measure 2 cm up from this edge and fold the paper down on this measurement.

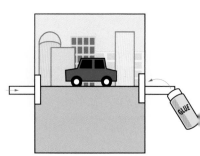

2. For the slide, cut a strip of thick paper 2 cm wide from the long edge of A4 paper. Make and glue a 'journey' item, e.g. a car or a boat, to the centre of the strip.

3. Put slide into the fold of the paper. Glue two small strips of paper to the sides, over the fold to keep the slide in place.

✏️ USE IT!

- Make a car shape for the slide. Ask the children to think about what essential things we need to take on holiday. List them in order of importance.

- Go over the well-known poem, 'The Owl and the Pussycat' with the class. Make the owl and the cat in a boat for the slide and write the poem in the space beneath, for this handwriting task.

- Make the wooden horse of Troy for the slide with the gates of the city drawn on the right side. Retell the story from the perspective of one of the soldiers hiding inside the horse.

Into space

1. For the base, fold an A4 sheet of paper in half lengthways. On the folded edge, cut a slot and a semi-circle as shown. Unfold.

2. Cut thick A4 paper in half lengthways. Glue a strip of paper to the top edge.

3. Turn the base so that it is landscape and put the slide on the back of the base (on the half with the slot and circle). Glue the ends of two strips of paper to the base to hold the slide in place.

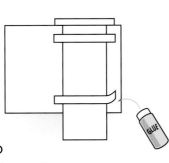

4. Turn over. Pull the slide down and draw the Earth through the circle. Make a rocket with a tab on the right side. Put through the slot to glue the tab to the back of the slide.

5. Push slide up and draw another planet through the circle.

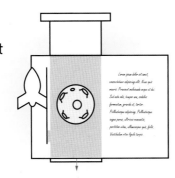

 USE IT!

- Complete all the artworks first. Write the spaceship captain's log on the base. What problems does he/she encounter while travelling through space and how are they solved?

- Write a letter from an astronaut on a space station addressed to a friend on Earth. What are the highs and lows of the job?

'Eat a healthy balanced diet' by Shaun (aged 7). Shaun has drawn a plate of unhealthy food and a plate of healthy food on his slide and has used a range of lettering and presentation styles in this health education project.

21 – Jointed paper mechanics

Surprisingly, paper is a very strong material. It can replicate and perform many kinds of mechanical objects and operations including pulleys, cogs and conveyor belts. Here are three different types of lever mechanism used in the book form.

Lifting arm

1. For the base, fold an A4 sheet of paper in half widthways. On the folded edge, cut two slots 2 cm long. Unfold.

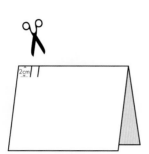

2. Fold the paper in half lengthways. On the folded edge, cut a 2 cm slot. Open the sheet. Make a small hole 1 cm below the centre of the sheet.

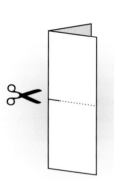

3. For the lever, cut a 4 cm wide strip from the short edge of thick A4 paper. Fold vertically 4 cm from left edge. On the folded edge, make a 1.5 cm cut.

4. Make the arm as shown. Note the 'dovetail' shape at the end of the arm. Fold the corners of the dovetail.

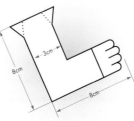

5. Put the arm through the middle slot on the base. Put a split pin through the arm and the hole on the base and open the split pin on the other side.

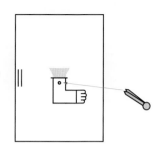

6. Turn the base over and put the lever through the vertical slots. Push the arm through the horizontal slot on the lever and unfold the ends of the dovetail.

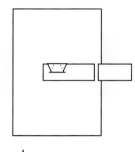

7. Turn over to front. Make and glue a fork to the hand. Pull and push lever to move the arm.

✎ USE IT!

- Draw a person on the base to go with the arm. Write a newspaper heading to match the mechanism, e.g. 'Billy eats his weight in sausages' or 'Martha just loves mountains of mashed potatoes'.

- A popular Victorian child's toy was a moneybox in which a hand lifts to place a coin into a person's mouth. Write about the most popular toys from the past and compare those of rich and poor children.

- Make the mechanism a person cleaning his/her teeth. Design an advertisement for toothpaste. How many different flavours does it come in?

Bird in flight

1. For the base, fold a thick sheet of A4 paper in half lengthways. Measure 7 cm down from the top and make a 1 cm cut on the folded edge. Measure 2 cm from the bottom and make a 1 cm cut on the folded edge. Unfold.

2. For the lever, cut a 2 cm wide strip from the long edge of thick A4 paper. Measure 4 cm from the top and fold.

3. Make the bird wing about 6 cm long. Put the lever through the bottom slot of the base and push the folded end through the top slot. Glue the wing to this end of the lever, about 3 cm from the end.

4. Note that the fold on the lever needs to be about 1 cm or so above the wing slot to allow the wing to rise and fall when the lever is pushed/pulled.

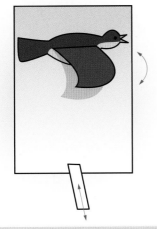

 USE IT!

- A Chinese dragon is the centrepiece of this project. Ask the class to use the Internet to find information about dragons in Chinese culture and mythology. Use different areas of the base sheet to record and group the findings.

- Ask the children to select a British bird for their artwork. Write about why birds migrate to Britain and where British birds migrate.

- Invent a bird-like creature with incredible moveable wings. Ask the class to imagine that they are curators of a natural history museum. Describe the appearance and peculiarities of this bird. Why is it so difficult to find?

'Restaurant' by Bryan (aged 10). Bryan used the space around the main drawing to add smaller artworks and text.

22 – Split level books

These books have been around for more than a hundred years. Some divide the body (or animals) into parts while other focus on the face. Whatever your approach, children love creating their own hilarious characters.

Make the basic split body book

1. Fold an A4 sheet of paper in half lengthways. Fold left and right edges to the centre. Unfold. Cut through middle of left and right flaps and fold inwards.

Split faces

1. Fold A4 paper in the same way as you did for the split body book. Cut left and right flaps into four or more equal parts and fold inwards. Keep the same proportions on each flap so that all the parts coordinate.

✏️ USE IT!

- On the front and back of the flaps and the middle panel draw and divide figures at the same waist measurements. Ask the children to see how many different types of dress and character type they can create.

- Use the suggestion above, but use famous people or styles of dress from different historical periods such as a Roman centurion or a present-day fire fighter for the figures.

✏️ USE IT!

- Discuss variations in eyes (including sunglasses), hairstyles (including headwear), etc. with the class. After completing the artwork, ask them to write a character profile of one of the characters the have created.

- Ask the children to take at least two of the characters and to construct a story around them. Start by giving them names that reflect their images.

- Add more split sections and subdivide other parts of the body. For example, break the bottom torso area down to show calf and thigh areas.

'Funny Faces' by Liam (aged 12). Liam was inventive in producing many contrasting facial features. He divided the head into five parts using a published split-level book as a guide. The face is seen from the front on the left and from the side on the right.

Split project book

1. Fold an A3 sheet of paper in half widthways and then lengthways. Unfold and turn so that it is portrait. From the left side, cut away a rectangle shape one third above and two-thirds below the middle crease as shown.

2. Fold the top half of the sheet forwards. Fold the front left panel to the right.

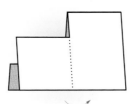

3. Fold the back left panel to the right

✏️ USE IT!

- Draw a village on the bottom panel, a town on the middle panel and a city on the top panel. Write about the communities that live in these areas on the blank spaces without artwork.

- Divide the book into creatures that live underground on the bottom panel, animals that live on the ground on the middle panel, and animals that live above the ground, such as eagles, on the top panel. You can use the same idea with sea creatures that live in the shallow, deeper and deepest parts of the sea.

23 – Secret garden books

Many of the book ideas in this book were inspired by Japanese origami or packaging design. Here, I use three ideas that were inspired by these sources. These forms are ideal for presenting poems and reflective writing.

Make the basic flower book

1. Make the largest square possible from A4 or A3 paper. Fold the corners to the centre.

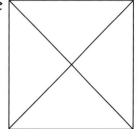

2. Turn over and fold the corners to the centre.

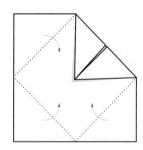

3. Fold the points of the triangles out as shown.

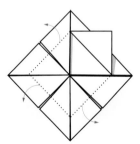

4. Write a poem in the centre.

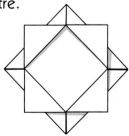

5. Turn over and fold the points of the triangles out. Write another poem in the centre.

✏ USE IT!

- Write a poem entitled, 'Only when…' For example, 'Only when the last tiger has been hunted will we realise that nature is beautiful'.

- Write a poem about a dream, entitled, 'Wouldn't it be great if…' For example, 'Wouldn't it be great if my bed where a sailing ship?'

Poems in a locket

1. Make the largest square possible from A4 paper. Fold all edges to the centre. Unfold. Cut away the corners and taper the flaps as shown.

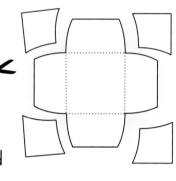

2. Interlock flaps in an 'over-under' pattern. Keep poems inside the locket.

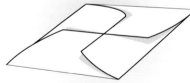

✏ USE IT!

- Write a poem entitled, 'When do I feel…' For example, 'When do I feel happy? When I feel like singing as loud as I can.' Lightly draw a background of images from your poem in coloured pencil crayon.

- Write a poem entitled, 'The Big If'. For example, 'If I were a rich person I would…' Write the poem on one side and illustrate it on the back.

Picture story box

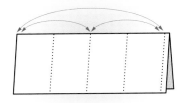

1. Fold an A3 sheet of paper in half lengthways. With the folded edge at the top, make a small fold on the right edge and unfold. Fold the left edge to this crease and unfold. Fold the left edge to the middle crease and unfold. Fold the middle crease to the right-hand crease and unfold.

2. Fold in half lengthways and unfold. Fold the top edge to this middle crease and unfold. Cut as shown.

3. Fold along creases into a box shape and glue the tab in between the paper on the other side.

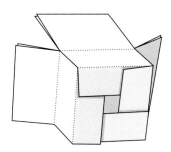

4. Interlock the flaps to form the box base as shown.

5. Open the front flaps. Make scenery out of paper and glue into the box.

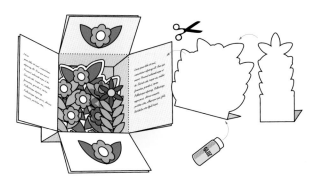

6. To store the box, you can fold the front flaps down like a lid. Or, you can unlock the base and fold the box flat including the scenery.

✏️ USE IT!

- This project is called, 'In my magic garden is a…'. Ask the children to write something different on each flap. This could be flowers that have magic properties, such as being able to dance, or a sunken garden that plays music whenever you enter it.

- Draw and add captions for a different flower on each flap. Include information about those flowers, such as the rose, that have special meanings.

⭐ Helpful tip: You will have to make some pages of writing/artwork upside down and others sideways depending on where they appear on the flaps.

'A Box of Wild Flowers' by Fahad (aged 10). This is a project on the cultivation of wild flowers. Fahad used the internet to research the subject and put different pieces of information on each of the sixteen flaps. Fahad also used the school library for a source of information for the illustrations.

24 – Containers for books

There is nothing like a slipcase or box to set off a beautifully made book. It also protects the book. There are many origami boxes — some needing more than thirty stages to make! These containers however are much more straightforward.

Make the basic origami case

1. Fold an A4 sheet of paper in half widthways. Put the folded edge at the bottom.

2. Fold the top half down to fold in half again. Fold the top corners down to the bottom and unfold to make diagonal creases. Fold the bottom corners up to the top and unfold to make two more diagonal creases.

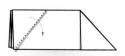

3. Where the diagonal creases end, fold left and right edges towards the middle panel.

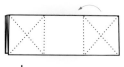

4. Unfold so that the paper is just folded in half again. Fold down the top corners on the front sheet. Fold up the bottom corners.

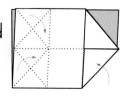

5. Fold the top half of the front sheet down.

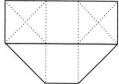

6. Pull the front section forwards to make the box shape.

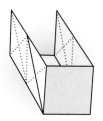

7. Bring the last section forwards to complete the box shape and tuck the triangular panels into the diagonal pockets on the sides of the box.

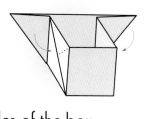

8. Put the box on its side with the opening facing forwards.

✏️ USE IT!

- For origami books (page 6), for this case, you will need to remove 6 cm from the long edge and 3 cm from the short edge of A4 paper before making the book. Use slightly thicker paper than usual, if possible, but not card, for the case.

- Make a decorative pattern on the paper before making the case. Use the theme of the book to help with this so that there is a repetitive design.

Slipcase

1. Fold an A4 sheet of paper into three vertical equal parts (page 5). Unfold. Fold the panel on the left behind the sheet.

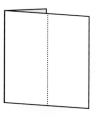

2. Fold the corners on the left forwards diagonally to the vertical crease. Crease horizontally as shown

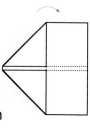

3. Fold the left panel forwards over the right panel.

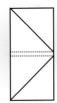

4. Pull the pocket forwards to make it into the slipcase.

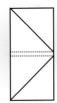

✏️ USE IT!

- To make an origami book for this case, you will need to remove 3 cm from the short edge and 10 cm from the long edge of A3 paper before making the book.

- Use the title of the book to go inside this case to create a repetitive design on the paper before putting the case together. Change the colour of the pen as you write each new title.

Book bag

1. Measure 3 cm down on the long edge of an A4 sheet of paper and fold down on this measurement. Measure 1 cm on the right edge and fold. Glue the left edge to the fold on the right edge.

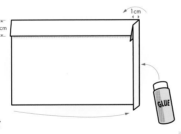

2. Measure 2 cm across on the left and right edges of paper. Fold forwards and backwards on these measurements. Measure 2 cm and 4 cm up from the bottom edge. Fold forwards and backwards and unfold.

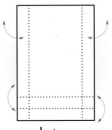

3. Tuck the left and right bottom corners inwards on the 4 cm crease, so that it looks like this.

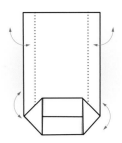

4. At the bottom, fold the top down on the 2 cm crease. Fold the bottom up on the 2 cm crease. Glue the edges down.

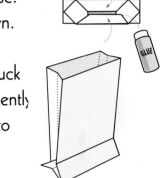

5. Open the bag and tuck the sides inwards. Gently push the bag down to look like this.

6. Make handles as shown and glue inside the top of the bag.

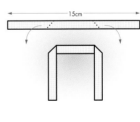
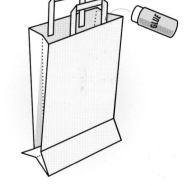

✏️ USE IT!

- To make the origami books for this bag, you will need to remove 4 cm from the short edge of A3 paper before making the book.

- Make this a present. Write a special greeting on the bag to the person who will receive your bag and the books inside.

- Invite the class to make a much larger bag using A2 paper. They can use this to store all the books they have made during the school year.

25 — Book stands

Displaying the books that the children make not only enhances the school environment, but gives all the effort they have put into their work a purpose. These stands give a professional touch to the presentation.

'A' frame stand

1. Fold an A4 sheet of paper in half widthways. Unfold. Fold in half lengthways and then fold in half lengthways again. On the folded edge, cut a right angle in the bottom half, 3 cm from the bottom of the sheet and 3 cm from the centre crease. Fold forwards and unfold. On the folded edge, 3 cm from the top, make a 3 cm cut.

This 'A' frame stand was made from thick drawing paper. The book on the stand, 'The Romans', was made by Lewis (aged 9).

2. Unfold so that the sheet is just folded in half again. Fold in half widthways. Push the flap through the slot to make the stand.

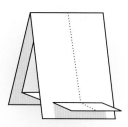

✎ USE IT!

- Use thick gift-wrap paper or experiment with collage or photomontage decorations.

- Making a stand for a book can be an integral part of the project. Use the book's theme to decorate the paper for the stand before making it.

★ Helpful tip: The stands on this spread are suitable for displaying an eight-page book made from A4 paper. For books made from larger paper, use larger and thicker paper for the stand.

Interlocking page stand

1. For the stand, fold thick A4 paper in half widthways. Measure 2 cm down from the top and cut 4 cm across from the folded edge. Do the same at the bottom of the sheet. Fold these sections forwards and backwards and unfold. Make 1 cm-deep cuts in the middle of these sections as shown. Open sheet.

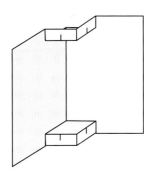

2. Pop the top and bottom sections inwards.

3. For the work, fold an A4 sheet of paper widthways in half. Measure 2 cm from the folded edge and cut 1 cm deep from the top edge. Do the same to the bottom edge. Open sheet.

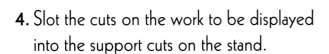

4. Slot the cuts on the work to be displayed into the support cuts on the stand.

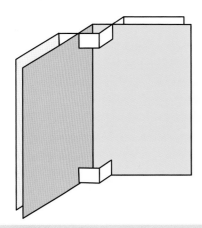

✏ USE IT!

- This is an excellent way of displaying poetry and single-page spread projects because you can fold the stand flat and use it as a partial cover.

- Use one colour for the paper for the work and a contrasting colour for the paper for the stand. Yellow on blue, or green on red would look effective.

Pop-up lecture stand

1. Fold an A4 sheet of paper in half widthways. Unfold and fold lengthways in half. On the fold edge, cut as shown and make two creases as shown. Unfold.

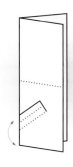

2. Fold the top half of the sheet behind the bottom half. Pop the flap outwards to form the stand.

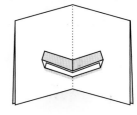

3. Place an A4 book on the stand.

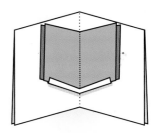

✏ USE IT!

- Make one large stand and use it to display the children's handmade books. Change the display regularly and label it 'Book for Today'.

- Attach several stands to a vertical display area, using pins and exhibit a range of books made by pupils on a specific theme.

Basic book 1

Enlarge the template to 127% to create an A4 template

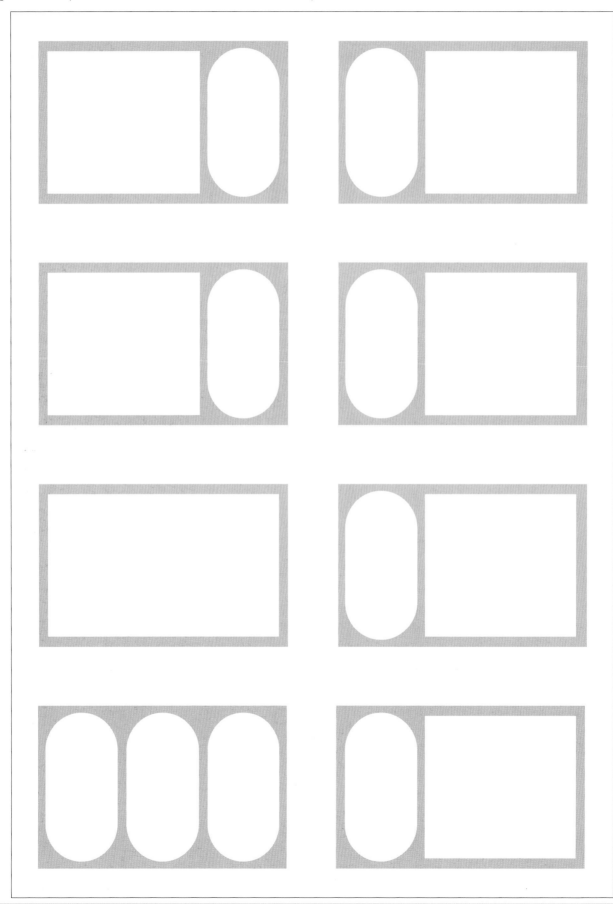

Basic book 2

Enlarge the template to 127% to create an A4 template

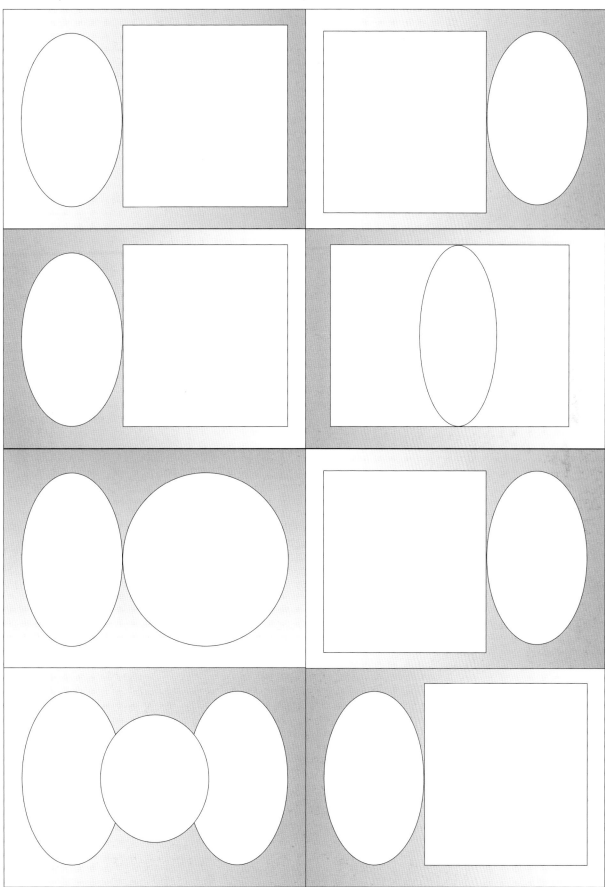

Pop-up origami book

Enlarge the template to 127% to create an A4 template

Locking theatre

Enlarge the template to 127% to create an A4 template

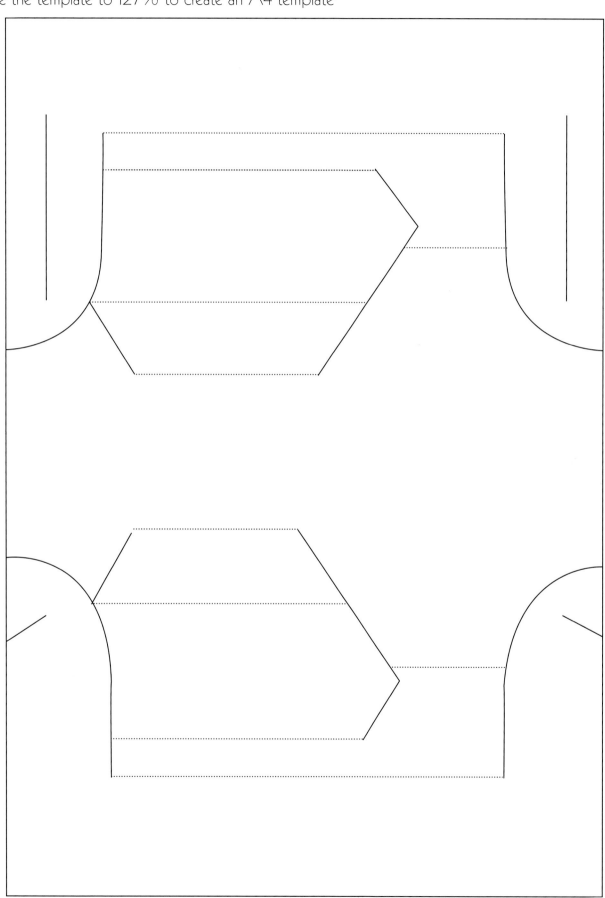

Suppliers and information

Paper

Increasingly, high street greeting card shops stock a range of high-quallity exotic papers like Japanese hand-made and machine-made papers decorated with embossing and plant inlays.

Budget Paper Supplies Ltd
Aborfield Mill, Helpston, Peterborough
PE6 7DH
0173 3252 868
sales@budget-paper.co.uk or
enquiries@budget-paper.co.uk
budget-paper.co.uk
Their catalogue covers a wide range of art, presentation and display papers, and they supply discount cartridge 130gsm paper in A1, A2, A3 and A4 sizes.

Yorkshire Purchasing Organisation
41 Industrial Park, Wakefield,
West Yorkshire WF2 0XE
01924 834 849
ypo.co.uk
For a wide range of watercolour papers to make and cover books

R.K. Burt & Co Ltd
57 Union Street, London,
SE1 1SG
020 7407 6474
sales@rkburt.co.uk
rkburt.co.uk

Check your local paper mills and paper manufacturers using the Yellow Pages for paper off-cuts and end-of-line offers.

Glue

Use Easy Clean PVA. This is a smooth, high quality and fast drying adhesive suitable for gluing paper and is available in 575 ml, 1 litre and 5 litre containers.
0845 120 4525
enquiries@nesarnold.co.uk
nesarnold.co.uk

Bookbinding and book art courses

The Society of Bookbinders organise regional meetings at which lectures and/or demonstrations are given. Visits to libraries, binderies and suppliers are also arranged.
societyofbookbinders.com

Designer Bookbinders list bookbinding courses throughout the UK.
designerbookbinders.org.uk

University of the Arts/London College of Communication run a wide range of courses in creative and traditional approaches to bookmaking.
arts.ac.uk

University of the West of England, Bristol
bookarts.uwe.ac.uk
The Department of Art and Design organises regular workshops and talks in the book arts.

The London Artists' Book Fair is held in November every year.
marcuscampbell.co.uk

The Leeds Contemporary Artists' Book Fair is held in March every year.
leeds.ac.uk/fine_art

At both the above fairs you can meet international book artists, including Paul Johnson, the author of this book, and see their work.

Education

The British Library
96 Euston Road, London, NW1 2DB
0870 444 1500
bl.uk

Look at the teacher's area of the website for curriculum resources.

The Book Art Project
Paul Johnson provides in-service courses for teachers both in the UK and the USA.
11 Hill Top Avenue, Cheadle Hulme, Cheshire SK8 7HN
0161 485 2174
pauljohnson@bookart.co.uk
bookart.co.uk

Pop-up books

Robert Sabuda and Matthew Reinhart are the undisputed masters of the pop-up book genre. Of their many individual and co-authored books published in the last decade or so, I would recommend Dinosaurs (Walker Books, 2005). Visit Robert Sabuda's official website to find out more about the man and his work:
rubertsabuda.com

At Mark Hiner's website you will find a wealth of information about how he designs pop-up books:
markhiner.co.uk